FOR YOU,
THE WORKERS
:-)

Copyright © 2019 Meeebooks

First published in 2019 by Meeebooks

www.meee.global
www.meeebooks.com
Email: info@ meee.global
Twitter: @Meee_HQ
Facebook: MeeeHQ
Instagram: MeeeHQ

Paperback ISBN – 978-1-9164134-3-6
.epub eBook ISBN – 978-1-9164134-4-3
.mobi eBook ISBN – 978-1-9164134-5-0

All rights reserved.

Sid Madge has asserted his right under the Copyright, Designs and Patents Act 1988 to be identified as the copyright holder of this work.

No part of this book may be reproduced or transmitted in any form or by any means, electronic or mechanical, including photocopying or recording, without the prior permission of the author.

Creative by SpiffingCovers.com

MEEE IN A WORK MINUTE
60 WAYS
TO IMPROVE YOUR WORKING LIFE IN
60 SECS

SID MADGE

ACKNOWLEDGEMENT

I dedicate this book to everyone
I have ever known and met,
as you have made and shaped Meee.

Sid Madge

CONTENTS

MEEE AND YOU AT WORK

If we consider where we spend most of our minutes, work will figure heavily for most of us. Whether we love our work life or hate it, we spend a large proportion of our time going to work, being at work or coming home from work. Even when we are not doing those things, work has a way of creeping into our thoughts – especially when we are under pressure or stressed.

According to *Gallup's State of the Global Workplace Report 2017*, a staggering 85 per cent of employees worldwide are not engaged, or are actively disengaged in their job. This indicates that a large proportion of employees either lack motivation and are less likely to invest discretionary effort in company goals or outcomes, or they are unhappy and unproductive at work, and liable to spread negativity to co-workers. Not only does this represent a stunning waste of human potential but it also means that work, for too many people, is nothing more than a necessary chore.

We all have good and bad days at work but when those difficult days string together or spill over into our personal lives, triggering arguments or making us feel worse, it's useful to have some tips and strategies at hand to break the spell and get back on an even keel. Sometimes, all we need is a little nudge to recalibrate our thinking so we can see a different perspective and access a different outcome or opportunity.

I know this to be true because I've seen it happen more times than I can count. It was this shift of perspective that led to the creation of the Meee Programme – a training and support network that focuses on the three E's – Education, Employment and Enterprise.

It all started when I was giving a talk to a class of teenagers at a school in Wrexham, north Wales. I used to be a brand consultant, and one of the questions I would ask my clients was, "What one word best describes your product or service?" In the classroom, I decided to ask the same question with a twist – what one word would the students use to describe themselves? The first response shocked me – a young lad raised his hand and said, 'weirdo'. Initially, I hoped he was being funny, but it soon became clear he wasn't. He explained that he felt as though he was always on the outside looking in and never really felt comfortable with others. Talking to the group in more depth, I was sad to discover that about 15 per cent of the youngsters thought of themselves as weird, abnormal, freaks or misfits. Too many felt anxious, insecure and self-conscious. Of course, growing up is challenging, and the teenage years are confusing at the best of times, but 15 per cent seemed too high to me.

For the rest of the session, we talked about who we are and the impressions we form about ourselves and what we are capable of. With a little encouragement and the odd nudge to consider their outlook differently, the whole class came to appreciate that often what they perceived as weakness, was the basis of their unique strength. Laughter began to lighten the mood as everyone was able to see a different point of view, or way of looking at themselves, that changed the way they felt for the better.

I was amazed, not just by the initial impression many of these young people had of themselves, but by how easily it was shifted, at least temporarily.

That session lit a fuse for me. I researched, read, studied and sought to develop more tools to help people change their perspectives so they could better understand who they are and what they are capable of. The result was the Meee Programme. The vision of Meee is to inspire each and every person to believe in themselves and what they can achieve. And, although it's called Meee, it's really about you and how you can improve your working life in a minute!

Meee in a Work Minute: 60 ways to improve your work life is a collection of life hacks, advice, insights, science, stories, short exercises or thought experiments and quotes that can help you improve your work life in a minute. (*Meee in a Minute: 60 ways to improve your life* is also available.)

Sometimes, all we need is a shift in thinking, which can present us with a new mindset, or point of view, or even trigger a more constructive attitude. We imagine change to be an endless uphill battle, but sometimes it can happen in a minute.

Meee in a Work Minute is designed as a permanent companion – keep it with you at all times.

Dip into it when you are about to go into an important meeting but don't feel in the right frame of mind, when you have had an uncomfortable conversation with a colleague or manager, or when you need to think differently and come up with solutions or new ideas. Dip in for a boost or just a little feel good magic.

I hope it helps you during the tough times, and allows you to celebrate the good times.

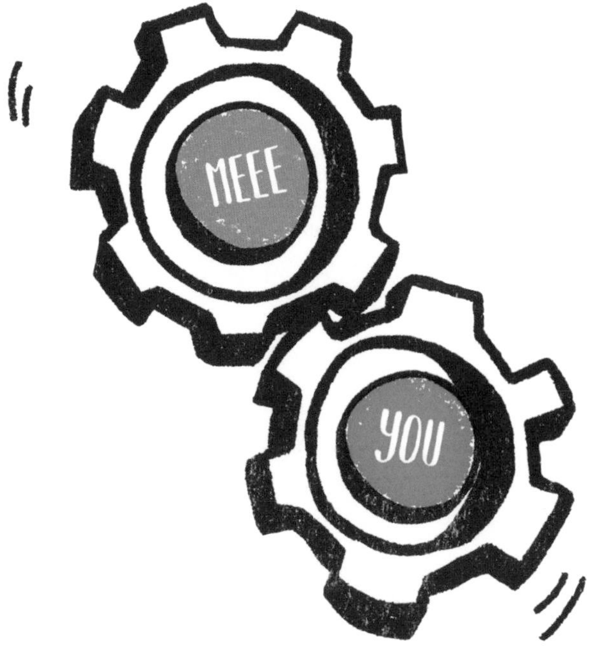

Me Mee Meee®

Be Amazing. Be Awesome. Be You.

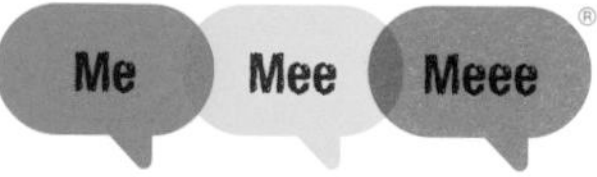

00:01

SMILE

Smiling can make you and others happy.

Roy T. Bennett

If I asked you to choose one word to best describe yourself, what word would you choose? Is it a positive or negative word? Why did you choose this word?

Add one extra smile a day. It doesn't take much and it doesn't cost anything. If we all added just one more smile a day, that would be over 65 million more smiles in the UK every day, and over 7.4 billion more smiles a day worldwide! What an amazing thought.

Some fun facts about smiling…

1. Smiling is contagious. Neurons in the brain have a synchronising feature that keeps you in sync with who are you speaking to. If they smile, you'll smile, and vice versa!
2. Smiling is good for your health. A genuine smile boosts your immune system by decreasing cortisol in your body. Even if you fake a smile, it will trigger

the release of endorphins which will reduce your blood pressure and make you feel better!

3. Smiling is good for your career prospects. Smiling shows your boss that you are engaged and easy to work with, which will improve your promotion prospects.

4. Smiling is a universal sign of happiness. People, regardless of language or culture, will recognise a smile.

5. Smiling is easier than frowning. A genuine smile involves your whole face, not just your mouth.

6. Smiling is an ability we were born with, and those that smile often live longer.

7. Smiling makes us look better.

Right now – smile. If you are on your own, think about something that makes you laugh or someone you love and are grateful for. Bask in your own smile. Or if you are with others, smile at the next person you meet. If we all practise smiling a little more, we could smile ourselves happier. Take a minute, go online and look up the poem *Smiling is Infectious*. It's a great poem by the wonderful Spike Milligan.

00:02

JUST TRY IT!

Trying is always enough.

Patricia Briggs

You'll probably have heard the encouragement, 'Just do it'! Instead, 'Just try it'. We are often asked to do new things at work, learn new skills or become better or more productive. This can feel daunting. We are often unsure whether we have the necessary skills or aptitude to pull it off. We wriggle, procrastinate and backtrack in the hope that the request be forgotten, or that it simply goes away.

But, what if we just tried? There is always a process from first attempt to proficiency, and it's never a straight line. The journey is littered with setbacks and embarrassing mistakes, and we may wish to go back to the way things were. But nothing stays the same forever, so embrace the change and just try. For example, we might be asked to migrate to a new computer system. It's annoying and confusing but if we just try, then try again tomorrow, and again the day after that, the system will become more familiar. Before we know it, it's second nature and we won't remember why we were so reluctant in the first place.

Take a minute to consider something that your colleague or boss wants you to do at work. Everyone is nervous when doing something for the first time. Just try. Get comfortable with the trying, be consistent in your effort and I guarantee you will be surprised by the results.

00:03

KEEP A JOURNAL

Writing in a journal reminds you of your goals and of your learning in life. It offers a place where you can hold a deliberate, thoughtful conversation with yourself.

Robin S. Sharma

We live in a world where we are encouraged to confront others and deal head on with the problems we face. Though, often, we don't fully understand those issue ourselves before we go roaring into a meeting, all guns blazing. This willingness to speak up or confront issues has merit, but only once we've done the personal work on ourselves to appreciate our own role in the dramas we are involved in.

Writing a regular journal can be useful and illuminating. It can lead to greater personal insight and development, rather than spending thousands on expensive courses or therapy. It allows us to consciously assess and make note of our mood and how we feel, and to trace those feelings back to their source. Doing so helps us better appreciate why we are feeling a certain way, and it helps us identify what is bothering us before we start a discussion with others. A journal is a written conversation with ourselves that can throw up some surprising truths, allowing us to see ourselves more clearly and honestly so we can engage genuinely with others.

Take a minute to consider what kind of journal you want to write. Depending on your focus, you might choose a work journal or a food journal, where you record what things you've done, things to do, what you eat and drink and how you feel as a result. These insights might help you change your behaviour. You might also prefer a family journal or a simple life journal, where you write about whatever is important to you in the moment.

00:04

HABIT ASSESSMENT

Your net worth to the world is usually determined by what remains after your bad habits are subtracted from your good ones.

Benjamin Franklin

When we think about habits, we usually think about our negative habits, such as smoking or eating too much chocolate. But there are also positive habits that can help us, like brushing our teeth twice a day.

What are your habits at work? Make a list of them and, alongside each one, note down whether it's a positive habit, or a negative habit that you would like to change. According to author Charles Duhigg, every habit, good or bad, is made up of the same process. First there is a trigger. It might be a time of day or a situation that happens every day at work, or something else. A routine is then triggered by that cue and, in the end, we get the reward the habit was designed to deliver.

Take a minute to watch Charles Duhigg's explanation of how habits form and how we can break them at **meee.global/MIAWM**. Once you've watched the clip, consider what triggers the habit you would like to change. What is the routine and what reward are you getting from the behaviour? Is the reward worth it?

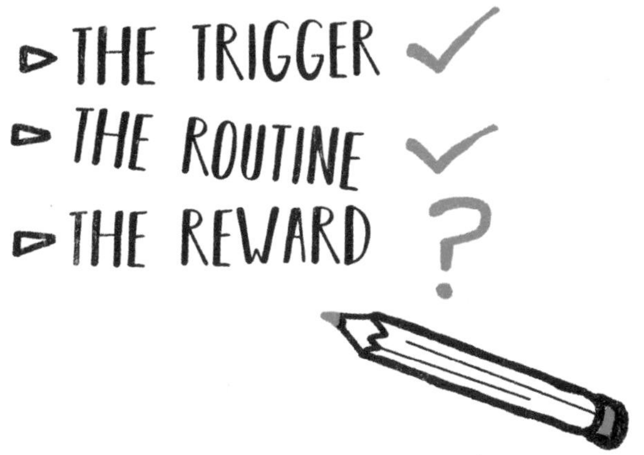

If the reward is not worth it, have a think about what you can exchange this failing routine for. Adapting behavioural patterns and breaking bad habits is far easier to do when we realise that a more constructive approach will bring about far more beneficial rewards. Remember that your net worth to the world will increase with every bad habit that you choose to remove from your everyday life. That has to be worth the change!

00:05

FIRST THINGS FIRST

The key is not to prioritise what's on your schedule, but to schedule your priorities.

Stephen Covey

In the 1920s, Ivy Lee, the father of modern public relations, received a call from Charles M. Schwab, CEO of Bethlehem Steel. Schwab was irritated by the low productivity of his managers and wanted to know how he could make them use their time more effeciently. Apparently, Lee offered to give Schwab the secret to time management that would solve his problems. All Schwab needed to do was implement the system for one week and then send him a cheque for what he thought the advice was worth. Schwab followed through and sure enough, the impact was almost immediate. He sent Lee a cheque for $25,000, which is about a quarter of a million dollars in today's money!

So, what was the advice? At the end of each day, each manager was asked to list their top six priorities for the following day and rank them in order of importance. Next morning, when they came into work, the managers were to work on the number one priority until it was complete, or no further action could be taken. Then they'd move to priority two and repeat the process.

One of the quickest ways to reduce stress at work is to focus on the most important stuff first and do that. This can also stop you becoming overstretched. Take a minute and skip to page 154 where you can to write down your priorities for work tomorrow and order them by importance. Tomorrow, when you go to work, start on that list and follow Ivy Lee's advice.

00:06

WHAT DO YOU VALUE?

Your beliefs become your thoughts,
Your thoughts become your words,
Your words become your actions,
Your actions become your habits,
Your habits become your values,
Your values become your destiny.

Gandhi

Our beliefs, thoughts, words, actions and habits become our values, which ultimately determine the quality of our lives. Money is a common *value* at work. We tend to take the job that pays the most. I remember being offered a job in Holland many years ago. I would be working with a global advertising agency and the salary was a significant jump up. I'd worked in Holland before and enjoyed it. On paper, it was a no-brainer. The weekend before I was due to leave, I spent some time with my daughter who was 10-years-old at the time. I asked her what she thought about me taking the job and she said, "I think it's a pants idea, Daddy." (For international readers, 'pants' is a UK colloquialism for 'terrible'). As soon as she said it, I realised that I thought it was a pants idea too.

VALUES VS

For some time I had felt that I wasn't doing what I was born to do, so why would doing the same thing for more money help that situation? I wasn't following my heart or doing work that aligned with my values. I didn't take the job in Holland in the end. Instead, I started the Meee Programme and I've never looked back.

Take a minute to think about what you really value. How would people describe you? Honest? Friendly? Hard working? Helpful? Selfless? These can shed light on your values. Alternatively, visit our website at **www.meeevalues.com** and do the values exercise. Once we understand our values, it's often easier to find work that aligns with them and we can find our groove.

00:07

IDENTIFY YOUR STRENGTHS

Don't let what you cannot do interfere with what you can do.

John Wooden

We can't all be rock stars, filmmakers or sporting legends, but we can recognise our innate abilities and gifts, and learn how to harness and utilise them for greater satisfaction and happiness at home and at work.

Unfortunately, the typical school system teaches us that value and ability sit neatly within subject areas and a set curriculum. If we are not very good at those subjects or we don't respond to the way they are taught, it is easy to assume that we don't have any strengths at all. But we all have our own abilities and strengths, which means we are better at certain things than most other people. Identifying what those strengths are can be liberating and exciting.

Take a few minutes to complete the Clifton-

Strengths Assessment, based on the work of Donald O. Clifton, widely considered the 'father of strengths-based psychology'. Drawing on over 50 years of research, Clifton created a language for the 34 most common talents and developed a questionnaire to help people identify the strengths they possess. It is available online and the questionnaire takes about 35 minutes to complete. You can opt for a detailed report on all 34 talents, but the shorter (and cheaper) version that focuses on your top five 'signature strengths' is sufficient and can really help you capitalise on them.

Working in a role that uses your strengths will make you more productive, happier and more successful. Without this knowledge, it can be too easy to accept jobs for all the wrong reasons. Knowing your strengths can ensure you find a role that suits your innate abilities, where you can thrive and add value.

00:08

NEUTRALISE YOUR WEAKNESSES

Focus on your strengths, not your weaknesses.
Focus on your character, not your reputation.
Focus on your blessings, not your misfortunes.

Roy T. Bennett

All the evidence suggests that there is no point wasting time and effort on turning a weakness into a strength. In their groundbreaking book *First Break all the Rules*, authors Marcus Buckingham and Curt Coffman documented the results of two Gallup research studies conducted over the course of 25 years. The research gave voice to over one million employees and 80,000 managers, and the conclusion was, "People don't change that much. Don't waste your time trying to put in what was left out. Try to draw out what was left in – that's hard enough!"

If you've done your strength assessment, you might know your strengths, but do you know your weaknesses? Take a minute to consider your weaknesses. Are they holding you back?

We may never convert a weakness into a strength but we can usually improve a little in that area so that we neutralise its negative impact. It's very hard to convert someone who hates being the centre of attention into a gifted public speaker, it's just not in their DNA. But with a little training or experience, that person may be able to do a presentation to a small group from time to time. If our weaknesses are causing problems, then we can usually improve them, just enough to stop them from limiting our career. After that, be more of who you already are and focus on your strengths.

00:09

WHAT'S YOUR VISION?

Vision without action is a daydream.
Action without vision is a nightmare.

Japanese Proverb

Do you really know what you want to do with your life? It's a big question and most of us don't know the answer. More often, we experience a sense of not being where we want to be, but we don't necessarily know where we should be instead. We take a job because we have bills to pay and families to provide for, without really considering if it's the best job for us.

What would you do if you knew you could not fail? What would your life be like? What sort of work would you be doing? Where would you live? Take a few minutes to really consider these questions. The answers might start to come together in your vision. A vision is your ideal destination. It might be very specific like, "I want to be a painter and live in the country," or it may be less definitive, such as, "I want to help others." Both are valid, whatever feels more real to you.

Once you have a sense of where you want to be, you can assess where you are now to determine how far from that vision you are. Break the vision down into smaller goals with timelines and milestones.

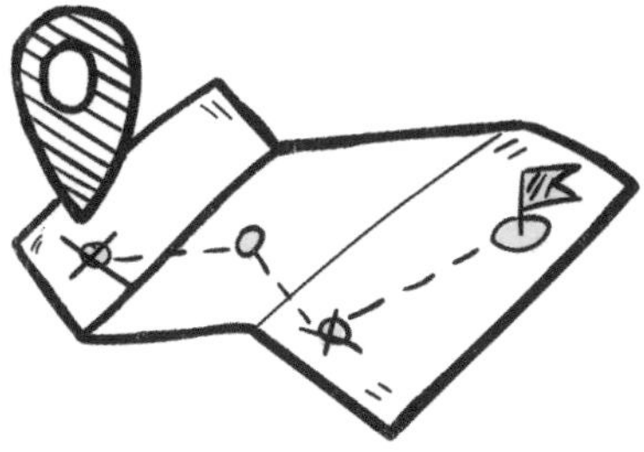

What action do you need to take now to achieve your vision? Think about the people that could help you, or the knowledge you will need to acquire to reach your destination. Without a vision to pull us forward, it can be very easy to drift off course and find ourselves at the wrong destination!

00:10

BEGINNER'S MIND

Real knowledge is to know the extent of one's ignorance.

Confucius

At work we are often expected to improve our performance, learn a new skill, a new way of working or even a new computer system. For some of us, the opportunity to learn something new is exciting, but we may also feel nervous or even irritated. What if we fail? What if we end up looking stupid?

Next time you find yourself in this position at work, instead of feeling nervous or irritated, try Shoshin. Shoshin is the concept of the 'beginner's mind' practiced in Zen Buddhism, which refers to an attitude of openness, anticipation and lack of assumptions and preconceptions when learning a new subject, even when that learning is at an advanced level.

Often, our ego gets in the way because we don't want to admit that we don't know something, especially at work where we *need* to know. But trying to learn anything from this position is like trying to fill up a glass of water that is already full. The beginner's mind suggests that we empty the glass first, accept that we know very little, and give ourselves permission to tap into the simple joy of exploring and discovering that children demonstrate so effortlessly. They are naturally curious and, as any parent will confirm, they love asking questions – endless, often bizarre questions! It's fun for them.

As adults, it's often the stuff we think we already know that stops us from learning something new or seeing something in a new way. As Zen master Shunryo Suzuki says, "In the beginner's mind there are many possibilities, but in the expert's, there are few."

Take a minute to consider how you could apply the beginner's mind to a learning challenge you have at work and try it out for a week. Be open, ask questions, have fun, make mistakes, laugh and try again. It's an easier and much more enjoyable way to learn.

00:11

ACTION IS THE BRIDGE BETWEEN VISION AND RESULTS

Vision without action is merely a dream.
Action without vision just passes the time.
Vision with action can change the world.

Joel A. Barker

Knowing where you want to go in your career, or what aspirations you have for your work life, is one thing; being committed to that journey is another. But, alone, they are not enough. Action is needed. That action doesn't have to equate to huge courageous leaps of faith. Small, deliberate and consistent action every day, and tiny tweaks to improve results, are more important and often more effective.

In the world of personal development, there are probably thousands, maybe hundreds of thousands of people who have attended weekend seminars, walked on fire or karate-chopped a block of wood and returned to their everyday life to make sweeping changes, such as quitting a job or leaving a relationship. Sometimes, such bold actions can work, but more often it backfires as the realities of life dampen the enthusiasm and water down the adrenaline. It's too much too soon without proper planning.

Action is critical for turning your vision into reality but it is often wise to temper that action with common sense and smart planning. This is especially true if other people will be impacted by your action. Action involves figuring out how to get from where you are now to where you want to be.

ACTION!

Take a minute to consider your vision. It's probably not something that can be achieved overnight. Put some planning time aside and really unpack the steps and stages that you will need to go through to realise your dream. Think about what you can do today to bring that vision closer to you? What milestones will you need to reach? Remember, without action there will be no results. But the action will probably be more effective if it's planned and diligently executed.

00:12

CONFIDENCE ON DEMAND

Low self-esteem is like driving through life with your handbreak on.

Maxwell Maltz

Confidence is central to just about everything in life. We have to believe that we will get the job, or that we deserve the promotion. This isn't about being arrogant or cocky, it's about mustering the confidence to give ourselves the very best chance. Of course, we don't always feel confident. Sometimes stuff happens and we lose our mojo. Can we get it back? Is there a spell or incantation that can deliver confidence on demand? Surprisingly, there is, although you won't need a magic wand.

Social psychologist Amy Cuddy ran some very interesting tests. The saliva from a group of volunteers was tested to establish their baseline levels for testosterone, considered the confidence hormone, and cortisol, the stress hormone. The group was then halved and each group was asked to perform a physical pose or body movement for two minutes, after which their saliva was tested again. Remarkably, those who had been engaged in a 'high power' pose experienced a 20 per cent increase in the confidence hormone and a 25 per cent reduction in the stress hormone. Those who had been doing a 'low power' pose experienced a 10 per cent reduction in the confidence hormone and a 15 per cent increase in the stress hormone.

Next time you need a quick hit of confidence, maybe before a job interview, nip to the bathroom and do a 'high power' pose for a couple of minutes. The easiest one to remember is the Superman or Wonder Woman pose. Stand up straight, shoulders back with your legs hip distance apart, hands on your hips. Look forward with your chin tilted upward and breathe deeply as though you have just arrived to save the world!

Check out Amy Cuddy's great Ted talk at **meee.global/MIAWM**. Also, take a minute to Google what the low power poses look like so you can avoid them!

00:13

MORNING MEDITATION

Science experiments have found that people who practice meditation release significantly lower doses of cortisol, known as the stress hormone.

Dan Harris

Stress is a common problem for many of us at work. Too much to do, looming presentations, performance reviews, deadlines... it can feel never-ending. But stress can be extremely bad for our health and well-being. High levels of cortisol, the chemical released by the body when stressed, has been implicated in many of the most common diseases we face today, including diabetes, high blood pressure, heart disease, cancer, depression and dementia.

Take a few minutes to try a morning meditation. You don't need to wear a kaftan, sit cross-legged or burn incense to meditate and reap its benefits. Just start your day with 10 minutes of silence. Focus on your breath. If thoughts arrive, just let them drift through your mind.

You might also want to check out mindfulness. Essentially, it's really just about bringing your awareness back to the here and now, and focusing on the present. It's definitely worth trying, to reduce stress levels. There are many free apps on meditation and mindfulness available online.

00:14

MAKE IT HAPPEN

Unless commitment is made,
there are only promises
and hopes … but no plans.

Peter Drucker

To achieve anything in life, we need commitment. Nothing worth achieving is easy. There are times when it would be easier to give up and relax. Every great accomplishment is met with obstacles along the way.

If you are clear about your vision you need to follow through on the goals and plans you have identified, otherwise nothing much will change. For our tomorrow to be different, we need to commit to making our today different. This is true in our professional life as well as our personal life, and our health.

Either do or don't do – eliminate try, might, should and could from your vocabulary. When we sincerely try something, we usually surprise ourselves. But, if we say, "I'll try," as a means of stopping the conversation, to stop someone nagging us or to quiet the critical voice in our head, this is as useless as not trying. If you have no intention of doing something, own it and say so. But if you are serious, then muster your commitment and make it happen. Take a minute to Google 'The Man Who Thinks He Can' by Walter D. Wintle. Read it, print it out if you can, and read it to yourself first thing in the morning and last thing at night.

Commitment is an invaluable ally on your road to success. Be prepared to work hard and make sacrifices. Commit to a specific goal and make it happen, but commit to yourself and your health too.

Take a minute to commit to one of the goals from your vision. Just start small and get used to following through on your commitments to yourself and others.

00:15

POSTTRAUMATIC GROWTH

Some people deviate radically from their previous path and, on the way, convert the worst thing that happened to them into the best.

David Feldman

In 1967, psychiatrists Thomas Holmes and Richard Rahe developed a list of 47 stressful events that could impact health and happiness. The assumption was logical: we become more stressed when bad stuff happens to us, and start accumulating stressful experiences such as a job loss, illness or divorce. We are also more susceptible to physical illness, disease and depression.

But the fly in their theoretical ointment was the fact that not everyone who experienced particularly tough life events was negatively impacted by them. On the contrary, some of those people actively flourished. This field of study is called posttraumatic growth or adversarial growth, and studies have shown that great suffering or trauma can actually lead to huge positive change. For example, after the Madrid bombings in 2004, psychologists found that many of those affected experienced positive psychological growth. A diagnosis of cancer and subsequent recovery can also trigger positive growth.

The people in many of these studies found new meaning and purpose from having survived something terrible. Instead of seeing their situation as a failure or a problem, they believed Nietzsche, who said ...

Take a minute to think about a difficult situation in your life. What positives could you pull from the pain? Get creative.Think of at least three positives that the situation has given you. It might not be fun, but if we can find the silver linings, we can often move on quicker.

00:16

BELIEVE IN YOURSELF

Believe in yourself! Have faith in your abilities! Without a humble but reasonable confidence in your own powers you cannot be successful or happy.

Norman Vincent Peale

At work, in business or as an entrepreneur, if you don't believe in yourself, your abilities or your ideas, then why should anyone else?

It sounds easy doesn't it – just believe in yourself. Of course, it's not always easy to do in practice. I believe that part of the reason for this is that we have been so thoroughly conditioned into the myth of success, we have forgotten or ignored how success is actually achieved. There is no such thing as overnight success. The media may label a musician that way to create a more sensational headline, but the reality is that the musician is likely to have been practising their craft since they were a child. They may have been playing gigs for free for years and providing music to birthday parties. Whenever they were asked to perform, they did. Eventually, that effort pays off and they are classed as an overnight success.

We have to accept that success in any area of life is the product of constant failure, of trying, failing, getting back up, dusting ourselves down and trying again. Belief in ourselves is the consequence of accepting this journey of continuous improvement, while recognising and owning the incremental improvements we make along the way. Often, we just have to change our perception.

Take a minute to think of a situation in your life where you didn't have self-belief. Is there any evidence to support your thinking? Has the situation improved over time? Are you better than you were a year ago? If so, own that and realise that every effort provides feedback. Feedback provides essential learning to help us realise how to improve next time.

00:17
BE YOUR WORD

Be Impeccable with Your Word.
Speak with integrity.
Say only what you mean.

Don Miguel Ruiz

We live in a very fluid, constantly connected world. As a result, plans have become more variable because technology allows that. When I was a child, there were no mobile phones. If I planned to meet my friends, we had to make firm arrangements to be at a certain place at a certain time.

Today, the availability of various messaging apps and social media means that we can change plans two minutes before we are due to arrive somewhere. Whilst this connectivity has delivered considerable advantages, it has also created some unintended consequences. Sometimes what we say and commit to doesn't really mean anything.

It's almost like we have forgotten how to say what we mean, and mean what we say. We might be fine to meet later at one moment of time, but what if we change our mind? This fluidity in our social life has spilled into our professional life. The results are not always positive and can impact our reputation.

Reputation is everything. As an individual, it's all we have. As a business, it's what makes our brand trustworthy. Build it. Work with integrity. Be honest. Be truthful. There is still something valuable in being your word; being known as the person that will follow through no matter what. The person that can be relied upon, regardless of change; to do what we said we would do when we said we would do it.

Take a minute to think about your work life. Have you let others down or changed arrangements at the last minute in the last week? Why? Commit to being your word for one month and see how that feels. See how much your stock goes up in your professional life.

00:18

GO THE EXTRA MILE

There are no traffic jams on the extra mile.

Zig Ziglar

Why are there no traffic jams on the extra mile? Because hardly anyone goes there.

It's a cliché, everyone knows what it means, but not many people are willing to put in that extra effort. Good enough is good enough. And yet, if you look at the world's millionaires and billionaires, they are almost always workaholics. They love what they do, they love the game of business and put in the hard work over many years before reaping the rewards.

Success, whatever that means for you, is not possible without perseverance, sheer determination and tenacity. Foster flexibility to work outside your own comfort zone in order to bring your dreams to fruition. Take extra time to meet with people and get to know those who can help you. Do your best to reciprocate the relationship so you can help each other.

Take a minute to consider your working life in the last week. Have you gone the extra mile or did you get to 'good enough' and stop? If you stopped short, think about why? If you pushed on to the extra mile, how did it feel? Were you proud of your accomplishment, and did it make you feel good, even if no one noticed?

00:19

JUST BE NICE (JBN)

Goodness is about character – integrity, honesty, kindness, generosity and moral courage, and the like. More than anything else, it is about how we treat other people.

Dennis Prager

Just Be Nice!

This might sound really obvious, but often, especially in the business environment, we are expected to be efficient or professional. Yet this doesn't always incorporate being nice. Why not? Being nice to others is just smart business.

Psychology Professor Robert B. Cialdini, identified six basic but powerful principles of psychology that direct human behaviour.

1. Reciprocity – people feel obliged to give back to others when they have received. If someone

is nice to us, we are more likely to be nice in return. If we are given a gift, we are more likely to give a gift back.

2. Scarcity – people attach more value to something that is scarce.

3. Authority – people attach more value to information that is delivered by a figure in authority; think of a doctor in a white coat.

4. Consistency – people want to appear consistent with what they have done or said in the past.

5. Social proof – if unsure, people will decide what to do by observing what others are doing.

6. Liking – people will do more for people they like.

Liking is the key one to remember here, although the others are also useful, especially for marketing. We will always do more and go out of our way to help someone we like or someone who has been nice to us. It makes business sense and it's also a more enjoyable way to go through life. Take a minute to think about your day. Could you have been nicer to anyone? Tomorrow, just be nice to everyone you meet, even if you feel they don't deserve it. Not only will it brighten their day, but it will make you feel better too.

00:20

LISTEN TO YOUR INSTINCTS

Your mind knows only some things.
Your inner voice, your instinct, knows everything.
If you listen to what you know instinctively,
it will always lead you down the right path.

Henry Winkler

Author Malcolm Gladwell explores instinct as another intelligence in his book *Blink*. He opens by telling the story of a marble kouros offered to the J. Paul Getty Museum in California. Supposedly, the marble kouros dated back to the sixth century BC, and was for sale for $10 million. Cautious but excited, the museum ran a battery of rigorous tests to verify its authenticity. When the piece was shown to the world's foremost expert on Greek sculpture, she dismissed it immediately.

She couldn't explain why but her instincts told her it was a fake. Another expert had the same visceral reaction. In the end, the museum bought the kouros, but it is still widely regarded as a fake.

Gladwell suggests that this instinctive gut response is 'thin-slicing': the ability of our unconscious to find patterns in situations and behaviour based on a very narrow slice of experience. Instinct is hugely undervalued in the modern world, especially in business. And yet, if we learn to trust our gut response, it can protect us from making poor business decisions and guide us down the right path.

Take a minute to consider when you were last conscious of your instinct. Do you trust your internal sense, or do you tend to squash it down and cover it up with head-based logic? Or do you trust it and then try to justify it with logic? Next time you are aware of your gut response, go with it.

00:21

BREAKFAST WITH A BOOK

To read is to fly: it is to soar to a point of vantage which gives a view over wide terrains of history, human variety, ideas, shared experience and the fruits of many inquiries.

A. C. Grayling

I'm a huge fan of A. C. Grayling. His book *The Meaning of Things*, changed my life and led me to the path I'm on now. I met him in June 2018 and was thrilled when he signed my copy of his book, and also endorsed *my* first book, *Meee in a Minute.*

I know, firsthand, the power of books, so start your day learning something new. Or set aside some creative time first thing. Instead of streaming your favourite TV show on the train to work, listen to or read a book.

Reading can be one of the first things to go when we get busy, yet it should be the last. Books allow us a new insight or perspective, a new way of looking at an old problem, or a creative way to consider more solutions. It's not just about reading the words on the page. As such, no two people reading the same book will have the same experience. What we get from each book differs, depending on our life experience and worldview. The information on the pages can mingle with the information that is already in our mind to create new thoughts and ideas that can spark imagination and creativity. We can learn from other people's mistakes so that we don't have to make them ourselves, and we can stand on the shoulders of giants.

Take a minute to consider where you could find 20 minutes a day. Could you get audio books and listen to them on your commute home. Could you subscribe to a book summary service where you only read a summary of the book? Check out the Blinkist app focused on non-fiction books. Most are available as written summaries to read, or you can listen to the audio summary, and they take 20 minutes for the whole book.

00:22
EMBRACE CHANGE

People will try to tell you that all the great opportunities have been snapped up. In reality, the world changes every second, blowing new opportunities in all directions, including yours.

Ken Hakuta

Change is inevitable. It's what makes us who we are, and it will determine who we are tomorrow. We can either resist change or embrace it, and allow the opportunities it can create to flourish.

Interestingly, as children, we adapt to change easily. We're far more adaptable when we're younger, but we seem to lose that trait as we get older.

Stanford psychologist Carol Dweck has studied our ability to deal with change and the failure and upset it can sometimes bring. She suggests that our ability to use change constructively comes down to mindset. And, according to her research, there are only two – fixed and growth.

We are all born with a growth mindset. We don't

second guess everything as we grow up, we just try stuff, fail, and try again. When we learn to walk, we don't consider the face plants and the falling down as failure, we just get up and try again until we master walking. But as we grow up and enter the school system, we find out about failure and we are trained into the other mindset – fixed. Those with a fixed mindset form a fixed idea of who they are and what they are capable of. As a result, they stop trying new things and they stop embracing change, which in turn closes down new opportunities and avenues for exploration.

How fixed is your mindset? Take a minute and complete the online mindset test at **meee.global/MIAWM**. Consciously choose a growth mindset until it becomes more familiar to you. Make a point of trying something new at least once a week.

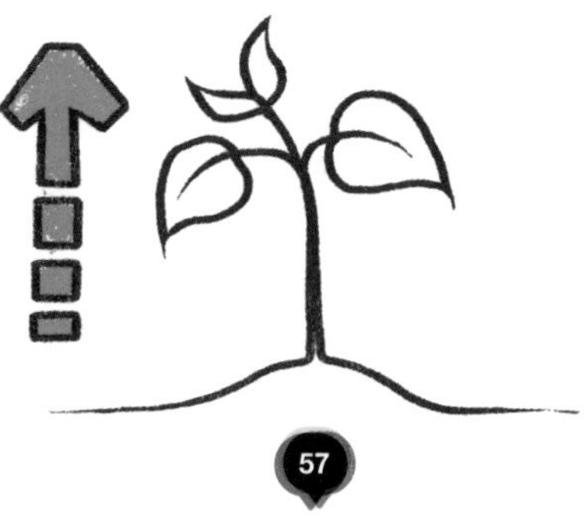

00:23

STEP BACK

If you change the way you look at things, the things you look at change.

Wayne Dyer

One of the quirks of human nature is our ability to normalise anything. It is an ability that has advantages because it allows us to deal with very difficult situations and find a way through. But it also has the capacity to rob us of appreciation and joy.

This normalisation process is often at least part of the reason why people stay in bad relationships or stay in jobs they hate. It is also part of the reason why winning the lottery doesn't always make people happy. They may be ecstatic for a few months, but over time, the win normalises and the issues that bothered that person before, perhaps minus their financial issues, resurface. We get used to stuff and we stop seeing it (good or bad) for what it is.

This happens to all of us. Take a minute to step back from your life as it is today. Cast your mind back to one year ago or five years ago or ten years ago. Shift your perspective. Taking account of a new timeline, consider how far you have come or what you have accomplished in that time. Are you amazed at how far you've come? What are you most proud of? Looking at our life from a different angle can sometimes allow us to push through that normalisation process and re-engage with what we are capable of.

Use that new insight to re-energise your efforts today. If you achieved all that in ten years, what could you achieve in the next ten? We almost always overestimate what we can do in one year, and vastly underestimate what we can do in ten.

Skip to page 156 where you can proudly jot down your achievements to date, as well as those you would like to see happen in the future. You'll be surprised at how inspirational this practical approach can be.

00:24

ARE YOU MOVING FORWARD?

The best career advice I've gotten is to stay focused, keep moving forward.

Micheal Ray Stevenson (Tyga)

Susan Jeffers, author of *Feel the Fear and Do it Anyway*, suggests that we constantly ask ourselves if what we are doing is moving us forward. It can be very easy in work or in life to just go through the motions. We get up, we sort out our family or the cat, and head off to work. We run through our to-do list, break for lunch and crack on with the list after a coffee and a sandwich. Then it's off home to sort out the family again (or the cat), a spot of TV to relax and then off to bed, only to repeat the whole process again tomorrow. Written like this, it can seem a little repetitive and depressing.

We need to be much more mindful about what we do during the day, and why we are doing it. Is what you are doing right now moving you forward? Yes, because you are reading this simple little book to get some ideas about how to improve your working life. But what about what you did this morning? Was that helpful to your end goals and moving you toward where you want to be? Or was it neutral or even negative – holding you back? What about what you did last night? Are you losing energy by engaging in battles with people at work that you don't need to engage in? Are you wasting time watching too much TV or streaming another episode of your favourite show, rather than taking constructive steps to move you forward in the direction of your dreams?

Take a minute to consider the last 24 hours. How much, as a percentage of that time, was spent doing something that moved you forward? Sleep definitely counts as it is necessary to recharge. But what about the rest?

00:25

BEEP

Sitting is the new smoking.

Dr James Levine

Dr Levine from the Mayo Clinic also says that, "Sitting is more dangerous than smoking, kills more people than HIV and is more treacherous than parachuting. We are sitting ourselves to death."

Researchers have found that prolonged sitting increases the risk of developing several serious illnesses, like various types of cancer, heart disease and type 2 diabetes. It has also been found that those who sit for more than six hours a day die earlier than people who limit their sitting time to three hours or less a day.

Of course, in the workplace, we are often sitting at a desk. What makes sitting especially challenging is that, like smoking, the damage it causes can't be reversed through exercise or other positive health habits. The only way to stop harming our health from smoking is to stop smoking, and the only way to stop harming our health from sitting is to reduce the time we do it.

So, take a minute to set the timer on your phone. If you are like me, your phone is never very far away. Set your watch to beep every hour.

When it does, get up from your desk and go for a short walk, or if you can't leave your desk, then stretch. If you do spend a lot of time sitting, you might also want to invest in a standing desk or at least try one out. Stick a treadmill under the standing desk and you could even exercise while working!

00:26

FIND THE MAJESTIC IN THE DOMESTIC

If a man is called to be a street sweeper, he should sweep streets even as a Michaelangelo painted, or Beethoven composed music or Shakespeare wrote poetry. He should sweep streets so well that all the hosts of heaven and earth will pause to say, 'Here lived a great street sweeper who did his job well.'

Martin Luther King Jr.

We all have to do things in life, especially at work, things we might not want to do or wish we could avoid. Life is never one exciting minute after another. Our social media feed might seek to put our best, more interesting experiences out into the world, but we all know that isn't how it works. And this is true for all of us, from street sweepers to rock stars or film directors. There are always boring minutes, dull minutes and disappointing minutes along the way.

That's just life.

But, research shows that people feel much happier when they are 100 per cent engaged in a task, even if the task is relatively boring.

Take a minute to think of a task at work that you dread or dislike. Next time you have to do this, instead of trying to get it over with as soon as possible, immerse yourself in it. If you need to do the housework for example, why not imagine you are Freddie Mercury dressed up in drag doing the hoovering in the video to *I want to break free*!

If you've never seen it, Google it! Whatever the task, it doesn't have to be a chore. Have some fun and do it to the very best of your ability. Each time you engage in the task, try to do it better than you did before. Pay attention to the details and decide to be positive and happy about your effort.

BREAK FREE

00:27

ATTITUDE = 100

If you don't like something, change it.
If you can't change it, change your attitude.

Maya Angelou

We often talk about attitude in our Meee workshops. What's really surprising about attitude is that, if you attribute a number to each letter where A = 1, B = 2 and so on for the whole alphabet, you are left with a total as shown below.

The word 'attitude' adds up to 100 exactly; that's not a coincidence. We need to give 100 per cent in everything we do in work and in life if we are to fulfil our potential and deliver the most value.

Take a minute to consider how much effort you give at work? Think about your effort level yesterday? On a scale of 1 to 100, where do you consider your effort level? If you are not operating at 100 per cent, why not? What do you need to do to shift your attitude and get closer to 100? Where is that missing effort going?

00:28

CREATE A 'TO-BE' LIST

Don't go on discussing what a good person should be. Just be one.

Marcus Aurelius

At work we often have so much to do: multiple competing priorities, and colleagues and bosses pulling for our time, attention and effort. We have traffic jams and late trains before we even get there, followed by what can sometimes seem like endless meetings or unrealistic timelines. Work can be tough and stressful, and sometimes we can get so focused on our to-do list, we forget about who we become as we seek to plough through the workload.

Take a minute to think about how you interacted with people at work yesterday? Were you kind?

Were you considerate and patient? Or were you needlessly short with someone, or even angry? If you had been on the receiving end of your own behaviour and attitude, would that have felt like a positive experience, or not?

We all have to take care of our to-do list at work and in life, but never forget about your to-be list.

Take a few minutes to create your to-be list now. What qualities and traits do you want to be known for? If someone was asked to describe you, how would you like them to describe you? Honest? Kind? Generous? Helpful? Inspiring? Choose one trait each day and resolve to demonstrate that trait for the day until it becomes second nature.

00:29

IDENTIFY YOUR WHY

He who has a why to live for can bear almost any how.

Friedrich Nietzsche

Mythologist Joseph Campbell once said, "Follow Your Bliss." In other words, find the things that make you happy and pursue that path. It's great advice but most of us have no idea what our bliss is. We leave school, and go to university or get a job based on nothing more than a few school grades. Or we take what's available and hope for the best. If we are lucky, we find a role that we like and we do well.

But what happens when we don't like our job? What happens when we hate our job but it pays the bills? Well, the first thing to remember is the quote from Maya Angelou from minute 00:27 (go and have a look to remind yourself). Then, identify your 'why'; you don't need to love your job, just love what it allows you to do. Does it pay for a hobby you adore? Does it provide for your family?

Does it allow you to study something you love in your spare time so you can retrain and move on to something you do love?

Take a minute to consider what your job allows you to do? If you don't love the job, what do you love that's made possible by the role? If this exercise proves to be especially difficult and you really can't find any benefits from doing your job, then do something about it. Change it. Update your CV, invest in yourself to reskill or retrain and find something you would enjoy more.

00:30
THE MIRROR

I'm a mirror. If you're cool with me, I'm cool with you, and the exchange starts. What you see is what you reflect. If you don't like what you see, then you've done something. If I'm standoffish, that's because you are.

Jay-Z

I love listening to podcasts. One of my favourite authors and podcasters is Tim Ferris. His podcast of an interview he did with Sir Richard Branson was awesome. One of the things that Branson said that really struck a chord with me was to always consider what you're doing and how it reflects on you? Branson suggests that, before we do anything, especially before making big decisions, we should consider how our actions will affect others and how that action will reflect on us.

What we do is never just about us.

Take a minute to think about what you have been putting out into the world, both in your personal and professional life. If what we experience is ourselves mirrored back, is that positive or negative?

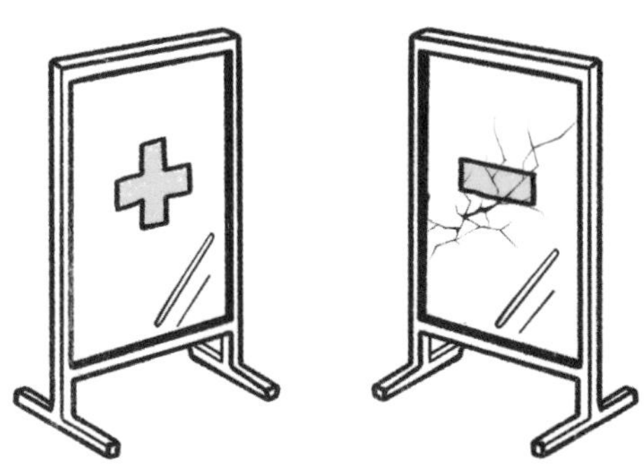

If you have more time, I would highly recommend that you listen to the full interview, where Branson talks about the importance of being a mirror – **meee.global/MIAWM**. You will also learn about how he coped with dyslexia, how his parents helped build his resilience, the behind-the-scenes stories of deal-making, his PR stunts, big wins, big losses and the habits (and life decisions) that he used to maintain high energy levels for decades.

00:31

180 THINKING

If someone gives you so-called good advice, do the opposite; you can be sure it will be the right thing nine out of ten times.

Anselm Feuerbach

One of the ways I occasionally relax is a good box set! One series I've particularly enjoyed is 'Billions', an American TV show starring Paul Giamatti and Damian Lewis. Loosely based on the real-life battles between a US Attorney and a Hedge Fund Manager, the series focused on the vendetta between Chuck Rhoades, played by Giamatti, and Bobby Axelrod, played by Lewis, an ambitious billionaire manager who Rhoades believes has bent or broken the rules. The plot is complicated by the fact that Rhoades' wife Wendy, played by Maggie Siff, is Axelrod's in-house performance coach, and doesn't want to be dragged into the battle.

In one scene, Wendy suggests her husband engages in 180 degree thinking. Her argument is that Chuck is getting nowhere with his current strategy to bring down Axelrod, so if what he is doing now isn't working, do the opposite and see if that works!

What a great idea! We often just double down on the same strategy and simply flog it harder, but if it's not working, working on it harder just makes it more wrong.

Take a minute to think about a strategy or way of working that you are currently following, but is not working. What could you do instead? Think of the exact opposite. If you are struggling to get the best from your team and you are berating them for it, try doing the opposite.

00:32
PUT YOUR HAND UP

When you clench your fist, no one can put anything in your hand, nor can your hand pick up anything.

Alex Haley

It is always wise to be open to life and say yes to experiences and opportunities that come along. It is only through this type of open approach that we learn new things and have new experiences that can lead on to different opportunities and adventures. School, for most of us, was a dull affair. We were never quite sure why we were learning certain things, and couldn't always see the connection between what has happening in the classroom and what was happening outside it. As a result, we march through the various ages, learning set subjects (or not), hoping to stumble across topics that capture our imagination. But that doesn't always happen. In fact, I believe more people leave school disheartened and disenfranchised than those who leave inspired and excited. Indeed, many of the people we meet through the Meee Programme are those that have been excluded or left behind by mainstream education.

In work and in life, put your hand up. Volunteer to do the extra work, stay late or learn the new computer system. Ask about available training programmes or courses. It's likely that your enthusiasm and willingness to work harder will be noticed. But these new experiences could also open doors for you, where you will find new skills or abilities that you never realised you had. Most businesses have a learning and development budget. Take a minute to consider what you would like to be better at and find a way to connect that to your work. Then approach your HR department to seek permission and funding. Most businesses are more than happy to support people who are willing to improve in a skill they need.

00:33

MANAGE YOUR TIME

The bad news is time flies.
The good news is you're the pilot.

Michael Altshuler

Did you know the average UK adult now watches around 24 hours of television a week, with one in 14 watching more than 40 hours a week. That's a full-time job, just watching TV. And nearly a fifth of survey respondents admitted watching TV at work! (If that's you, refer to minute 00:32!)

Whatever your TV habits, combine them with other screen time such as time spent on social media or browsing the internet and you'll find it uses up a huge chunk of time that could have been spent on more fulfilling activities. Spend your time wisely. We tend to spend a lot of time on senseless things, like excessive TV, shopping or social media, which only serve to distract us; they don't contribute to our happiness. In fact, there are many surveys which show that excessive use of social media is making us unhappy. It is too easy to compare ourselves to other people who, according to their Facebook feed, have a perfect life. It's rarely the reality.

Take a minute to consider how much time you spend watching TV, on your phone, tablet or computer, doing nothing of any value, every day. Commit to reducing screen time by at least an hour a day. Instead, swap out that screen time with some learning or outdoor time. Read a book, or go for a walk while listening to a book. You could also tackle something you've been avoiding from your to-do list, or get some exercise.

00:34

WHO DO YOU ADMIRE?

We tend to become like those whom we admire.

Thomas S. Monson

There are many people (and animals) that I admire, often for different traits. For example, I admire Professor A. C. Grayling, Freddie Mercury, Peter Cole (my art master), Jonny Barnes (see **meee.global/MIAWM**), Caravaggio, Steve Jobs (see **meee.global/MIAWM**), my mum and dad, Laura Bell, my partner, my three wonderful children and my dog Bilbo, who often saves my life.

Who do you admire? When we are asked this question, we often immediately think about famous people or bigname success stories, leaders or others who have changed the world. But we can also admire people closer to us; perhaps a teacher at school who gave that extra attention that made a difference to you. Or perhaps a colleague or boss that you found particularly inspiring and supportive. Take a minute to think of the role models in your life: the people who taught you something important, even if you never met them personally. They might be alive today, or they might be people from the past.

Consider each person in turn. What are the values you admire in them? What flaws or weaknesses did or do they have? Also, consider what they manage to achieve despite those flaws. Do you admire them a little more for that?

Are there any similar values or traits in the people you admire? Reminding yourself of the qualities and achievements you admire in others can help you make better decisions while finding the right way forward for yourself. Plus, taking the time to recognise their flaws only reminds us that no one is perfect, yet we can all manage to achieve something worthwhile.

00:35

FIND YOUR TRIBE

If they criticise you before they cheer you on, they are not your people. Simple.

Nikki Rowe

Our first tribe is our family, but that relationship is not always straightforward. Ironically, it can be our first tribe that casts doubt on or questions our dreams and aspirations the most, sprinkling a little fear into the conversation just to keep us from making a fool out of ourselves or making a 'mistake' that we might regret later.

As we grow up, we meet new people. Most of us make friends at work and our colleagues become our new tribe. If we are lucky, those people become our support network and have a positive influence on our lives, and vice versa.

Take a minute to consider who your tribe is right now. Is their influence positive or negative? Do you spend more time complaining and wallowing in a problem together, or do you focus on the future, making changes where necessary and enjoying the adventure? If you resonate more with the former, then you may need to recalibrate your tribe so that you find a more like-minded community: people who are committed to and passionate about the same things you are; people who are positive and bring out the best in you; people who support your dreams and inspire you to be the best version of you, you can be. Find that tribe.

00:36

CHOOSE HAPPY OVER MONEY

There are two ways of being happy. We either diminish our wants or augment our means.

Benjamin Franklin

If you want to live a happy life (and let's face it, who doesn't), it's important to set the right goals. We live in a fast-paced world where just getting by can be challenging. Depending on where you live, paying rent can eat up a large proportion of your income. Getting on the housing ladder can be virtually impossible. Bills and an escalating cost of living mean that we are almost constantly stretched financially, especially if we are on minimum wage, as so many people are. We assume that the solution is to chase a better-paying job, get a second job or get promoted and make more money. But is that really the right direction for you and your family? Possibly not.

Maybe Brendon Grimshaw had the right idea. In 1962, he purchased an abandoned tropical island in the Seychelles for £8,000. In the seventies, he quit his job as a stressed-out journalist in England and became the island's permanent caretaker. Grimshaw lived a happy life on the island for decades, planting hundreds of mahogany trees and turning his island into a wildlife refuge for animals, such as the giant tortoise.

Take a minute to think about this, and also consider Benjamin Franklin's sound advice. It's very easy to get on the hamster wheel of life, where we run ourselves ragged trying to meet our escalating needs. Why? Could we move to a cheaper area or somehow get off the hamster wheel and live a simpler life? Could we reduce what we need to earn and focus on our happiness, rather than simply making more money that disappears on stuff we don't necessarily need or value?

00:37

POWER OF GIVING

We make a living by what we get.
We make a life by what we give.

Winston Churchill

According to a 2008 Harvard Business School study, when we give to others, it makes us feel better about ourselves, which in turn makes us happier. It's as good for the giver as it is for the receiver. Despite believing that spending money on themselves would make them happier, participants discovered that giving to others also made them feel better. Happiness expert Sonja Lyubomirsky found similar results of increased happiness when her study participants performed five acts of kindness each week for six weeks.

Neuroscientist Jorge Moll and his colleagues at the National Institutes of Health found that people who give money to a good cause end up happier because the altruism activates regions of the brain associated with pleasure, social connection and trust, while creating a warm glow effect. His 2006 study showed that the reward centres in the brain are firing at a higher rate in altruistic people than in those who remain stingy with their cash. This in turn releases endorphins that result in the positive feelings known as the helper's high.

In the work setting we rarely give money, unless donating to a colleague doing a charity event. But the act of giving is, as Professor Lyubomirsky discovered, not just about giving money. It can also be activated through giving time, support, kindness and assistance. There are countless opportunities to help others in the workplace.

Take a minute to think about your last week at work. Did you see a colleague struggling with deadlines or an increased workload? Do you have spare capacity in your own workload? If so, perhaps you could offer to help that person? If you see someone struggling, offer your support. You never know where your actions may lead. Not only will it feel good, but you may also make a new friend.

00:38

INCENTIVE x 3

Call it what you will, incentives are what get people to work harder.

Nikita Khrushchev

What incentivises you?

According to the authors of *Freakonomics*, Steven Levitt and Stephen Dubner, "There are three basic flavours of incentive: economic, social and moral." In a work setting, and depending on the role, many businesses try to motivate their employees through economic incentives such as bonuses. However, social science has proven that money is a fairly poor motivator, especially in roles that require creativity and problem-solving.

The best incentives are the ones that combine all three flavours – economic, social and moral. Social incentives refer to the fact that human beings are inherently pack animals; we are social and we are motivated to feel as though we belong. Moral incentives relate to our desire to do the right thing. Of course, what 'doing the right thing' actually means will vary for each person, and their level of human development.

Take a minute to consider what you want to achieve in your career? If your aspirations revolve around making a set amount of money or breaking some new record in your bonus payment, it's unlikely that you will feel particularly inspired. It may be that you can muster the effort needed occasionally, but it's incredibly hard to maintain. However, if you can also recruit social and moral incentives into your aspirations, you will find it much easier to consistently maintain motivation to move toward your dreams. Consider how your goals allow you to meet your social needs, while doing the right thing.

00:39

DON'T TEAR DOWN – BUILD UP

How would your life be different if …
You walked away from gossip and verbal defamation? Let today be the day …
You speak only the good you know of other people and encourage others to do the same.

Steve Maraboli

The workplace can be a chaotic and stressful place sometimes. We might be asked to work with people we would prefer not to work with. Perhaps we are put on a team with colleagues that irritate us, or we find working on a project a slog because another colleague isn't as efficient as we might like them to be.

These challenges are not always easy or pleasant to work through, but complaining about it to others won't help anyone. We might feel momentarily superior, or even laugh about the screw up with work mates, but it's not helpful, to us, or the other person.

We never know what is going on in someone else's life. We never know the personal struggles they are having to deal with. The most constructive approach is to assume that everyone is doing the best they can with the resources they have at that moment. If those resources are not good enough, then find a solution; perhaps offer additional support or training.

Openly criticising or mocking others says more about us than it does about them. Build people up, don't tear them down. If that's hard for you to do, then stay silent. As my granny used to say, "If you can't say something nice about someone, say nothing at all."

Take a minute to consider your conversations at work over the last few days? Have you built people up or torn them down? Commit to sticking with encouragement or silence tomorrow, and see how you feel?

00:40

DEVELOP KEYSTONE HABITS

Small wins fuel transformative changes by leveraging tiny advantages into patterns that convince people that bigger achievements are within reach.

Charles Duhigg

Research indicates that doctors have a hard time convincing overweight people to make sweeping changes to their lifestyles, but when patients focus on developing one keystone habit, such as keeping a meticulous food journal, other positive habits start to take root as well.

These keystone habits, if identified and developed, have the power to create small wins that unlock a cascade of positive behavioural changes. According to Duhigg, author of *The Power of Habit*, keystone habits create a chain reaction that causes a beneficial ripple effect that can positively influence and change other areas of your life.

All keystone habits share three distinct characteristics:

1. They deliver a sense of achievement.
2. They act as fertile soil from which further positive habits can grow.
3. Their accomplishment creates added energy and increases confidence which can act as an additional springboard into more positive habits.

Exercise is an example of a keystone habit. Regular exercise, even once a week, can kick-start our desire to make positive changes in other areas of our lives, such as eating healthier, spending less on junk food and increasing overall level of productivity, while reducing our expenses and levels of stress. Sleep is another keystone habit, as getting enough sleep can also make us more productive, improve our communication and increase our likelihood of eating better.

Take a minute to consider what keystone habit you could develop that could trigger additional benefits. Finding ways to change lots of things can be daunting, but if changing one thing can cause a chain reaction all by itself, then identifying that keystone habit just makes sense.

00:41

WHO'S IN CONTROL?

Technology makes it possible for people to gain control over everything, except over technology.

John Tudor

Technology has delivered significant benefits to us both personally and professionally. It allows us to communicate with people all over the world in real time for next to no cost, and it offers access to huge amounts of information. We can find things, share things, buy things, sell things, learn things and change things with the help of technology. But those benefits can easily tip into drawbacks if we let technology control us, rather than the other way around.

Technology will always come with default settings that benefit the creator of the business who is selling or providing the technology or platform. We don't have to accept them blindly. Take a minute to go into the settings of the technology or social media platforms you use most frequently, and take back control. Consider turning off the notifications that pop up every few minutes, the ones that derail your train of thought. You can also unsubscribe from whatever companies are inundating your inbox with emails that add little or no value to your life. In fact, a good step right now might be to unsubscribe yourself from everything and then add yourself back to the small number of blogs, apps and podcasts that do deliver benefit to your life. Services such as **Unroll.Me** can help.

It is also wise to simply turn your phone off and put it in another room when you want to get some serious work done. Even when you're not in the middle of a project, scheduling daily *unplug time* will benefit your creativity. There are also tools and apps designed to help you improve your productivity, such as *Focus, RescueTime* and even the *Facebook News Feed Eradicator* plug-in. These can help you avoid internet-based distractions for extended periods of time.

00:42

WEAR SUPERHERO CLOTHING!

Being a superhero is a lot of fun.

Chris Hemsworth

Bizarre as it may sound, wearing a superhero T-shirt under your work clothes might just improve your performance.

Research conducted by Professor Karen Pine and her colleagues at the University of Hertfordshire, found that students wearing plain T-shirts obtained an average of 64 per cent when put through mental agility tests. Students who wore Superman T-shirts scored, on average, 72 per cent on the same tests. Similar improvements were also observed when a student wore a white coat while doing the tests.

Professor Pine noted that, "When wearing a Superman T-shirt, the students rated themselves as more likeable and superior to other students. When asked to estimate how much they could physically lift, [they also] thought they were stronger than students in a plain T-shirt, or in their own clothing."

According to Professor Pine, the results also showed that people's mental processes and perceptions could be *primed* by clothing, as they unconsciously embody the symbolic meaning of the clothing. Grounded in cognitive psychology, priming is when an environmental feature, (what someone is wearing in this case,) temporarily activates or primes mentally represented concepts, such as attitudes, behaviours, emotions, goals, memories, stereotypes and traits. In the study, the superhero T-shirt and the white coat allowed the respondent to adopt the perceived traits or abilities of Superman, or a doctor.

Take a minute to think of an upcoming occasion or event where you would benefit from feeling more capable, stronger or more superhuman. When getting dressed for that occasion, wear a superhero T-shirt or underwear and take on their gifts for a day. It might sound silly, but the mind is a very curious thing. Besides, what have you got to lose?

00:43

THINK LIKE DA VINCI

The noblest pleasure is the joy of understanding.

Leonardo da Vinci

Leonardo da Vinci was a polymath. In other words, he knew a lot of stuff about a lot of stuff. One of the ways he achieved this was by intentionally seeking out people who knew about things he was interested in, then asking them about it. Da Vinci kept notebooks which have thankfully survived. They were full of notes to himself about topics he wanted to investigate, such as, "Ask Benedetto Portinari by what means they walk on ice in Flanders." He was also insatiably curious, with reminders to himself to find out about a goose's foot and a woodpecker's tongue! Da Vinci knew that the fastest way to learn anything was to ask someone who was knowledgeable about it.

More recently, this approach was employed by Hollywood producer Brian Grazer, in what he calls his 'curiosity conversations'. In an effort to accelerate his learning and enjoy a good chat with someone interesting, he sought people in science, medicine, politics, religion, the arts, technology etc., to better understand those areas. These informal discussions often sparked his creative imagination, which led to new ideas that he would then convert into a movie or TV show. Grazer racked up 43 Oscar nominations and countless blockbusters, including, ironically, *The Da Vinci Code*, so it obviously worked!

Take a minute to consider something that you would like to know more about, or need to better understand for work? Who do you know, at work or outside work, who might know more about that subject? Approach them and invite them out for a curiosity conversation.

00:44

NO ONE EVER LISTENED THEIR WAY OUT OF A JOB

There's a lot of difference between listening and hearing.

G. K. Chesterton

We focus on the importance of listening in the employment section of our Meee Programmes (Education, Employment and Enterprise). We show two great TED talks, one from radio host Celeste Headlee (see **meee.global/MIAWM)** on the 10 ways to have a better conversation, and the second from Julian Treasure, who I used to work with (see **meee.global/MIAWM**). Definitely worth listening to both.

In his talk, Julian reminds us that, although we spend 60 per cent of our time listening, we only retain about 25 per cent of what we hear.

Why? Is it because we aren't really listening at all, or is it because we are too busy thinking about what to say next? Sometimes, it's because of the various filters (values, beliefs) and distractions that are around us.

One of the things that Julian talks about, which I think is really interesting, is the notion of listening positions, which we teach in our programmes. You can try this with a friend or colleague – it only takes a few minutes. All you need to do is explain to the other person what you ate for breakfast or describe your commute to work. The other person must listen from different listening positions. First have them listen from *bored (disengaged)*. Then repeat the process and have them listen from *interested (attentive)* or *curious (inquisitive)*. Try again with the other person listening from maybe *angry* or *irritated*. Swap so that both of you experience giving and receiving the information from various positions. Notice how dramatically your listening position influences your mood and your ability to actually hear what is being said, and retain the information.

Being able to listen and absorb information is incredibly important at work, for getting on in life and adding value. Use this simple exercise to remind yourself of the importance of listening from the right *place*.

00:45

FEAR VS LOVE

I believe that every single event in life happens in an opportunity to choose love over fear.

Oprah Winfrey

One of my favourite speeches ever was the one delivered by Jim Carrey during his commencement address to Maharishi University of Management's class of 2014. Carrey was also awarded an honorary degree in recognition of his significant lifetime achievements as a comedian, actor, artist, author and philanthropist.

In his speech, Carrey says, "Life doesn't happen to you, it happens for you. How do I know this? I don't. But I'm making sound, and that's the important thing. That's what I'm here to do. Sometimes, I think that's one of the only things that are important. Just letting each other know we're here, reminding each other that we are part of a larger self."

For whatever reason, Carrey's speech resonated with me. I think that at least part of the reason is because we regularly work with people who have not been dealt a great hand by life. Often, they don't feel part of that larger whole. They're forgotten and regularly disenfranchised and yet, without exception, once they start to choose love over fear, something miraculous happens.

Take a minute to determine where you spend most of your time. Grab a clean sheet of A4 paper and fold it in half lengthways. On one side write Fear at the top. On the other side, write Love. Right now, what you do fear the most? Think about your work and personal life. Repeat the process for what you love. Looking at the list, where do you spend most of your time? Make a conscious effort to shift away from fear into love. Also, watch Jim Carrey's speech at **meee.global/MIAWM**.

00:46

GROSS NATIONAL HAPPINESS

Gross National Happiness is more important than Gross National Product.

King Jigme Singye Wangchuk of Bhutan

Bhutan is a landlocked country in South Asia, and home to fewer than a million people. In 1972, the King coined the term 'Gross National Happiness' as a quantitative measure of the collective happiness of the residents of Bhutan, prioritising their overall well-being over commercial gain or productivity. This idea was radical at the time, and sadly, is still radical today. Although, more and more people recognise that we simply can't carry on placing profit and commercial growth above the well-being of the planet, or the people, plants and animals living on it.

It can be disheartening to observe the world and all that is going wrong, from excessive corporate greed to climate change, political uncertainty and division, but pioneers have seen the writing on the wall. In 1968, Robert F. Kennedy spoke at the University of Kansas and said, “Too much and for too long, we seem to have surrendered personal excellence and community values in the mere accumulation of material things.”

I couldn’t agree more. The things that make you happy are not things. We do a ‘What does success mean to you’ exercise, where we ask groups in the Meee Programme to write or draw their answers. What’s amazing is that most people cite happiness, family and achieving goals as being most important to them. Wealth may be mentioned as money is necessary, but increasingly, we recognise that it can’t buy us happiness. Take a minute to consider what you are prioritising in your life? What are you measuring? What makes you happy? Do more of that.

00:47

MIND THE GAP

The silent gap between your thoughts is your window to the cosmic mind.

Deepak Chopra

Anyone who has travelled by train or on the London Underground will be familiar with the message to pay attention and not fall through the space between the train and the platform.

The concept has also been co-opted as a reminder to pay attention to our lives so we don't fall through the space between all our competing priorities. Life is busy. In fact, many of us have made an art out of being and remaining busy. We define our worth and value by how busy we are. Though, being busy doesn't allow for the gap or pause to appear and guide us in unexpected ways. In music, the pause or gap between notes is as important as the notes themselves. Likewise, it's the silence or gaps in

PAUSE

conversation that allow the exchange to really connect. This is also true of life.

Take a minute to consider what consumes your time? What thoughts keep you awake at night? If we want to live happy and productive lives, we need to learn to heed our life-sustaining rhythm and disengage at regular intervals. At work, this means taking a relaxing break every one and a half hours or so. Go for a leisurely stroll through a nearby park for fifteen minutes. Stop thinking and just enjoy the gap.

00:48

REALISTIC OPTIMISM

Realistic optimism involves enhancing and focusing on the favorable aspects of our experiences. Examples include being lenient in our evaluation of past events, actively appreciating the positive aspects of our current situation, and routinely emphasizing possible opportunities for the future.

Sandra L. Schneider

In a frantic effort to maximise our time, we tend to choose useful activities over enjoyable ones. We assume that that is the best use of our time, but constantly prioritising work over play, or useful over enjoyable, can have powerful negative consequences.

We derive positive emotional energy from doing things we enjoy or find relaxing. In fact, it's positive emotions, like pleasure, feeling challenged, experiencing adventure and seeing opportunities, that fuel our sense of well-being and optimal performance.

Of course, in the course of our daily lives, we

can't always focus on the things that we find enjoyable. Sometimes we just have to get stuff done, especially at work. That's where realistic optimism comes in – viewing the world as it is, while simultaneously working toward our desired outcome. Realistic optimism helps us keep our sights on the target, even when things go awry. It allows us to accept that we will not always be successful in what we attempt. Rather than focusing on the shortcomings or shortfalls, appreciate how far we have come, find the positive aspects of our performance and use these to reduce self-doubt and maintain the motivation to try again.

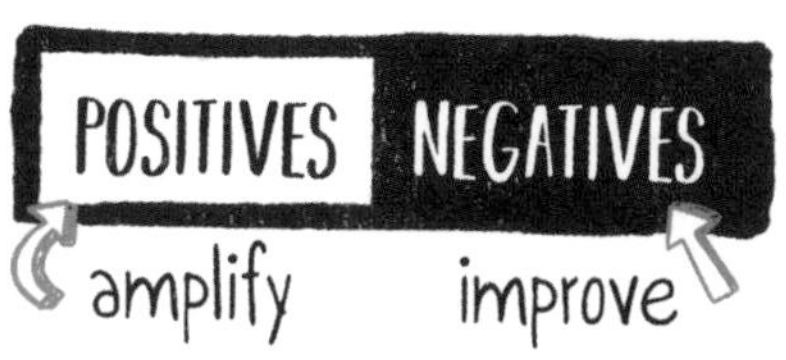

Take a minute to think about a project or task at work that didn't go according to plan, or one that didn't work out quite as well as you'd hoped. What did work well? What parts of the task did you enjoy? Find ways to amplify those positive aspects and take pride in them while also working to improve the parts that did not work so well.

00:49

COMPASSION FOR OTHERS

Love and compassion are necessities, not luxuries. Without them, humanity cannot survive.

Dalai Lama

We tend not to think about compassion in the workplace. It's something we might feel fleetingly after watching some natural disaster unfold thousands of miles away on the nightly news or when we hear a sad story, but it's not an emotional response that we are encouraged to experience or demonstrate often, especially in business. Business, so the thinking goes, has no room for compassion or sentimentality. Sometimes, in the business environment, people treat others negatively, and they even have a phrase that they believe exonerates them from the fallout – "It's not personal, it's just business."

What nonsense. Business is people. People make up the workforce. Suppliers, customers, shareholders – they're all people. As such, compassion for others should be a priority at work, not an afterthought.

The antidote to being self-absorbed is to look

outward with a compassionate, open heart. Compassion means being sensitive to those around you and acknowledging the distress of others. Being empathetic is, in fact, hardwired in human nature. This might come as a surprise given the dog-eat-dog world we live in. But, German researchers found that chimpanzees and young children without knowledge of learned social practices, will go out of their way to help a companion in need.

Interestingly, being compassionate can also be good for business. A 2011 study from Michigan University that focused on compassion in the workplace, found that showing compassion improved company performance levels and profit margins, and increased employee happiness. Only by being kind to each other can we thrive both as individuals and as a society.

Take a minute to think of your colleagues. Do any of them appear to be struggling? Reach out and ask them. Do what you can to help their situation and offer comfort and support.

00:50

COMPASSION FOR SELF

Remember, you have been criticising yourself for years and it hasn't worked. Try approving of yourself and see what happens.

Louise L. Hay

It's not just about showing compassion to others. Quite often, we are our own harshest critics. We berate ourselves for mistakes made or things not achieved. Whatever we try, it's never quite good enough. This self-criticism is rather destructive and unhelpful. It can trap us in negative habits and rob us of enthusiasm and optimism for the future.

One way to really appreciate the destructive tendencies of the inner critic is, ironically, to give it a voice. Write down how you feel. Writing is a great way of becoming more aware of how you are feeling, and to become more compassionate toward yourself as a result. Let your true feelings flow onto the page. Write whatever comes to mind, even if it would be hurtful to others if they read it. Don't censor your thoughts and feelings – just write. Also, use a pen and paper rather than typing on a computer, tablet or phone, as it will make the experience more personal. Writing about how we feel can have positive, long-term health effects. Recent studies have shown what writers have always known – that you can regulate your emotions by writing about them. When we are stressed or unhappy, writing about it can help defuse the negative impact on our mental and physical well-being.

Take a minute right now to write about something that is bothering you. Initially, write for five minutes, then build up over time. Write for as long as you want once you get into the habit of doing so. If you are worried that someone might find what you've written, then destroy whatever you write after each session. What's written is not important; the expression is. Often, once expressed, the negativity will just melt away and you will feel different, allowing compassion for yourself and others to flourish.

00:51

EMBRACE UNCERTAINTY

Embrace uncertainty. Some of the most beautiful chapters in our lives won't have a title until much later.

Bob Goff

Life is uncertain. They say the only thing that is certain is death and taxes. We can't seem to avoid those two aspects of our lives, but everything else is up for debate. It's easy to assume that we would be more productive if we knew exactly what the plan was, and then simply executed that plan. But a Harvard experiment found that that wasn't always the case. The study found that painters were less creative when working on commission. They felt constrained, even if the commission was welcomed because they needed to deliver something that matched the purchaser's expectations, rather than experiment to see what might emerge from the creative process.

In another study, psychologist Franck Zenasni discovered that people who were willing to accept uncertainty, were significantly more creative. They thrived on the ambiguity and were willing to press on if the solution in place wasn't perfect.

Ironically, one proven way to embrace uncertainty is to institute routine, which builds consistency and acts as *certainty anchors*. Too much uncertainty is chaos and that can be quite damaging, so maintaining some regular routines during particularly challenging times can liberate our minds, freeing them to come up with genuinely creative solutions. When we are under pressure or facing impossible deadlines, our routines are often the first things to go. We stop visiting friends or going to the gym because we don't have time. This is a mistake.

Take a minute to consider your current routine. When you are feeling particularly uncertain, maintain your routines. If you don't have any, institute a few. Even if that means you leave your desk every day for a few minutes and walk around the block. It may feel counterintuitive, but routine can help us embrace uncertainty and unlock greater creativity.

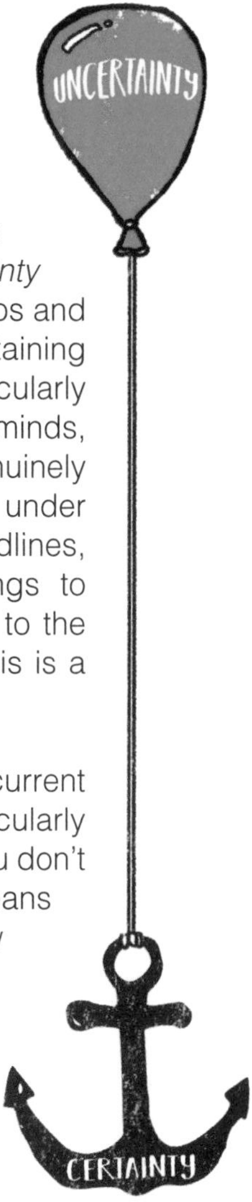

UNCERTAINTY

CERTAINTY

00:52

DECISIONS ARE NOT RATIONAL

When dealing with people, let us remember we are not dealing with creatures of logic. We are dealing with creatures of emotion.

Dale Carnegie

I always find this quite amusing. In business, we are expected to leave our emotions at the door and become logical, rational human beings – almost machine-like. Emotion of any sort is frowned upon in the workplace; a demonstration of weakness or having lost control. The problem with that theory is that it's just not true. Human beings are emotional beings. Emotion is simply physiological signals and transmissions flying around the body, and they are happening all the time regardless of gender. It is impossible for us not to experience emotion. More than that, emotion is central to our decision-making capability. We couldn't leave them at the door, even if we wanted to.

Our understanding of decision-making started with Phineas Gage. Gage was a railway construction foreman in the 1840s, who suffered a traumatic brain injury when a metal pole was blasted into his head. Amazingly, he survived, but his character changed completely. He could answer basic logic problems but was unable to make decisions anymore.

Having thoroughly researched the accident and reconstructed the brain injury, neuroscientist Antonio Damasio believed this was because the metal pole had severed the connection between the brain's logic centre and its emotional centre. According to Damasio, we need emotion to make decisions. In fact, our emotions are the deciding factor for 95 per cent of our decisions. So, rather than *thinking and acting*, we generally *feel and act*. Damasio's work led him to believe that human beings aren't "thinking machines that feel," but rather, "feeling machines that think."

We need to embrace our emotions rather than turn them off or pretend they don't exist. Next time you have a decision to make, listen and take a few minutes to really tune into and feel your emotions. Pay attention to how you feel about the decision. Trust that emotion and use it to make the best choice.

00:53

PYGMALION IN THE WORKPLACE

High achievement always takes place in the framework of high expectation.

Charles F. Kettering

There is a famous experiment called *Pygmalion in the Classroom*, which was conducted by Harvard social psychologist Dr Robert Rosenthal. At the start of the year, Rosenthal tested 18 classes of primary school children using non-verbal intelligence tests. Twenty per cent of the kids were then identified as being *intellectual bloomers*, meaning their teachers could expect to see significant intellectual gains from those children. The teachers were told of the results but the students were not.

A year and a half later, all the children were tested again. The scores revealed that all the children previously labelled as bloomers *had* increased in IQ points over the rest of the group. Initially, the teachers were not surprised by these results, until they were told that the children identified

as intellectual bloomers had been chosen randomly, not based on their previous test results. The only explanation for the increase in IQ was that the teachers' expectations of those children changed *their* behaviour toward them, and made them better teachers to those children.

The teachers pigeonholed each child from the outset – smart or average – and this assumption, regardless of its validity, influenced their teaching style and behaviour toward each child, which ultimately affected the outcome. This is known as the *Pygmalion Effect*, named after a play by George Bernard Shaw. It refers to the fact that people will rise or fall to meet expectations – their own, and other people's.

Take a minute to consider what you expect from each of your colleagues, and what they expect of you. Change your perspective so that you expect the best of yourself and others. You'll be surprised at what might happen. Take a few more minutes to watch the YouTube clip about the experiment at **meee.global/MIAWM**.

00:54

DO ONE THING WELL

It's better to do one thing well than ten things poorly.

Heather Hart

I've borrowed this from David Hieatt, the co-founder of the Do Lectures and Hiut Denim Co. David's story is similar to mine in that he worked in the creative industry, big job in London, realised he wasn't that happy, and decided to move back to his hometown in Wales, in his case, Cardigan. First, he started a clothing company that he eventually sold, then he started The DO Lectures where various creatives were invited to give lectures on their business or idea. This, in turn, inspired others to go out and follow their passion.

Do one thing well was a saying David's father, a merchant seaman, followed all his life. It's proving particularly useful in David's latest venture, the Hiut Denim Company. Cardigan used to be home to Britain's biggest jeans factory, turning out 35,000 pairs of jeans every week and employing up to 500 people. The factory left town in 2001, but the skill didn't. If there is one thing that the people of Cardigan know how to do well, it's make jeans. And Hiut Denim is about getting the town back to doing that one thing well.

It's a brilliant mantra and reminds us all to do whatever it is that we're doing, well. Don't take on too much, so that whatever you're doing, you're doing it well.

Take a minute to consider what one thing you do well. Maybe you do several things well. Do you use that skill every day? If not, why? Resolve to do your one thing well every day.

00:55

SAY THANK YOU

Appreciation can make a day – even change a life. Your willingness to put it into words is all that is necessary.

Margaret Cousins

Show appreciation for others. Don't be cryptic or assume that someone will know that you are grateful for their help or support. Speak up! Say thank you.

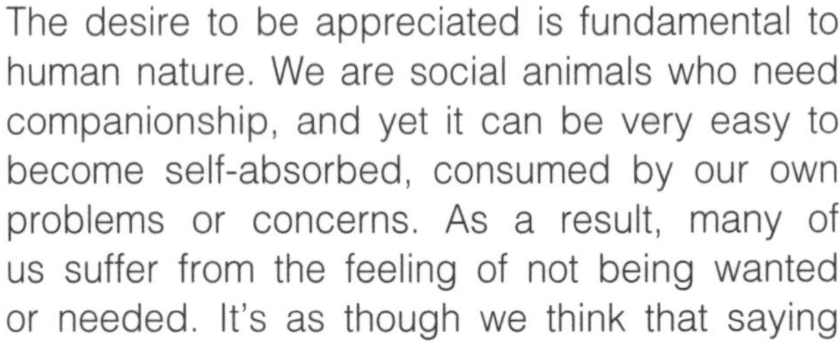

The desire to be appreciated is fundamental to human nature. We are social animals who need companionship, and yet it can be very easy to become self-absorbed, consumed by our own problems or concerns. As a result, many of us suffer from the feeling of not being wanted or needed. It's as though we think that saying thank you will make us vulnerable, and we will have shown weakness; that we needed the other person's help in the first place. We all need help in life from time to time. Saying thank you is just an honest acknowledgement and appreciation of that fact.

Take a minute to think about who you could say thank you to. Perhaps you should have done so already but you've just never found the time. Have any of your team at work been putting in extra effort? Or does a family member deserve some appreciation? Don't assume that others know that you are grateful for their effort, input or support. Commit to at least one sincere thank you every day. If you enjoy it, go for more. But make sure they are sincere. Say why you are grateful as this will feel more authentic to others and to you.

00:56

SAY SORRY AND MEAN IT

An apology is the super glue of life.
It can repair just about anything.

Lynn Johnston

On the subject of speaking up and voicing how we feel, sorry is also a very powerful word and should be used as often as is genuinely necessary. Along with thank you, we often feel reluctant to express regret or say we are sorry. Again, it can make us feel as though we are accepting blame or admitting that we were wrong; not something any of us enjoy.

Though, saying sorry is not just about admitting guilt or wrongdoing. Sometimes it's just acknowledging that what we did caused someone else's distress. Expressing that can often break the spell and allow for an open, honest and healing conversation. What's interesting is that we usually know when we should apologise. We feel *off*. We know that what we did wasn't an expression of our best self, but we often justify our actions and stay quiet. Remember, two wrongs don't make a right.

Take a minute to consider a situation at work that has become complicated or fraught. Have you treated someone badly in your family or social group? If someone else had behaved the way you behaved, would you be upset? If so, make amends. Say sorry and mean it. For real authenticity, articulate why you are sorry rather than just saying sorry; it will feel more real to the other person. There are very few situations in life that can't be fixed, or at least greatly improved, by a sincere apology.

00:57

NOTHING IS EVER HOPELESS

A little more persistence, a little more effort,
and what seemed hopeless failure
may turn to glorious success.

Elbert Hubbard

There is wisdom in this bit of truth: no situation is hopeless. There are people in the world who have already overcome every conceivable situation. Some people have overcome unimaginable suffering and, even when they felt hopeless, they found a way to carry on.

Hopefully we won't have to survive a terrible event or life-changing trauma, although bad things happen to good people all the time. For most of us, we will just have to muddle through life as best we can. We will have to deal with the usual ups and downs of work, life, relationships and money worries. But nothing is ever hopeless and nothing is ever permanent. Stay the course, keep putting one foot in front of the other. Persevere a little longer, muster a little more effort and just keep going. Hold on to the hope that tomorrow will be better.

Take a minute to give yourself credit for where you are today. What hardships and losses have you endured? There may have been muck and bullets along the way, but you've made it this far. Congratulations. Now, how do we get to the next bit? What can you do today to make sure your tomorrow is better, easier, more enjoyable, healthier or even happier?

00:58

MAKE YOUR OWN LUCK

I am a greater believer in luck, and I find the harder I work the more I have of it.

Thomas Jefferson

It's easy to look at others who are enjoying good fortune and believe it's because of luck. Sometimes it is. But even lottery winners had to do something; they had to buy the ticket.

It might be comforting to assume that luck is the chance attribute that separates those that succeed from those that fail, but it's rarely true. Was a colleague lucky to get promoted or had they been putting in the extra effort for months? Was James Dyson lucky that he stumbled across the bagless vacuum cleaner and became a billionaire? No, luck had nothing to do with it. Dyson worked tirelessly, investing his life savings to try and find a prototype that worked. The one that did eventually work was prototype number 5,127. He spent 15 years in a process he called 'purposeful failure'.

In life, there is winning and there's learning. Losing is just a lesson you learn so you can improve your chance of winning next time. And, it might not be sexy, but the harder we work the luckier we become.

Take a minute to think of something that you've lost enthusiasm for? What about giving it one more go, and maybe another after that. What worked well and what could you improve next time? Break it down if you can, to assess your strengths and weaknesses so you can make adjustments that will improve the result.

00:59

DIAL DOWN THE OVERWHELM

Many of us feel stress and get overwhelmed not because we're taking on too much, but because we're taking on too little of what really strengthens us.

Marcus Buckingham

The first option is to review minute 00:05. Sometimes we can dial down the stress and overwhelm by being clear on our priorities and working on what needs doing first.

The second solution is to take charge of the number of decisions we need to make. When we have too much on our plate, it can be easy to suffer from decision fatigue. Have a look at the decisions that are contributing to your overwhelm, and decide *when* you need to make them. We can feel overloaded by too many decisions, but when assessed, many of them can be delayed without much of an impact. This will give you some thinking space. One of the reasons Steve Jobs wore the same thing every day was to reduce the number of decisions he made.

The final option is to be honest with yourself about the work you do. Stress and overwhelm is rarely just about the amount of work we do, it's usually more about the type of work we do and whether we enjoy it, or are challenged by it.

Take a few minutes to really consider your job as it is right now. Do you enjoy it? Do you enjoy it sometimes? If so, why do you enjoy it sometimes and not others? Does the role inspire you or challenge you? Would you enjoy it more if you could include more flexible working? If so, ask if that's possible. Or is it just that you hate your job but don't really know what to do about it? If so, it's time for change. Update your CV. Decide what role you are looking for and what you are prepared to do to secure it. Life is too short – make the move.

00:60

CREATE A GRATITUDE RITUAL

Enjoy the little things, for one day you may look back and realise they were the big things.

Robert Brault

The secret to being grateful is simple – choose to be grateful. Then choose again. If you forget, just decide to be grateful when you remember.

No one said life was easy or fair. It can be very tough sometimes. We lose people we love, relationships break down, our health fails or we have to watch as a loved one suffers, we lose jobs and struggle with money worries. But, there are also beautiful moments and wonderful people who love us and have our back no matter what we face. The trick is to focus on those things – the good things we can be grateful for – however small.

Taking the time to bring to mind everything that we are grateful for at the end of every day, triggers a human quirk known as the *peak-end rule*. According to Nobel prize-winning psychologists

Amos Tversky and Daniel Kahneman, our appreciation of an experience is dependent on the most extreme point in the experience (either good or bad) and the end of the experience. We don't view the whole experience – we take snapshots of the high (or low) and the end, and draw conclusions from those moments.

If you end your day by calling to mind all the things you are grateful for, from that day, you trigger the *peak-end rule*. It's like a band playing their most loved song at the end of a show; everyone leaves the concert on a high because the end was excellent. We can mimic the same result by ending our day on a high via a gratitude ritual.

Take a few minutes as you get ready for bed to remind yourself of all the things you are grateful for in your life. You can either write them down or just speak them aloud.

You must live in the present, launch yourself on every wave, find your eternity in each moment. Fools stand on their island of opportunities and look toward another land. There is no other land; there is no other life but this.

Henry David Thoreau

I hope you have enjoyed this book as much as I've enjoyed writing it.

To discover more about the Meee Programme and how you can get involved visit us at **www.meee.global** or email us at **hello@meee.global**

To take the next stage on your journey watch our free webinar at **www.meee.global/webinar** for many more practical hints and tips.

MEEE IN A WORK MINUTE TESTIMONIALS

Here are some testimonials from some of the wonderful people who have read our first book *'Meee in a Minute'*, attended our talks, courses and workshops.

From our first book 'Meee in a Minute'

"A fantastic little book to keep close and dip into. Full of practical exercises and inspiring quotes to help everyone feel more positive and get the most out of life! Thoroughly recommend."

"Just have to share an unexpected benefit to my family of 'Meee in a Minute'.

"My daughter Charlotte had one of the two hard copies I bought, I felt she needed a bit of self belief that she can have a career as a midwife although currently stay at home mummy to Alex (10), Max (7) Zack (6 months)."

"Alex is a very bright boy, popular and kind, but gets bored easily and is probably borderline ADHD. He came home from school on Monday and the teacher said he had been disruptive. Charlotte asked him to think about his behaviour and to do the pros and cons list. They then had a discussion about the adjectives he had used, and she showed him the book. He is an avid reader but never this type of book. He sat absorbed for half an hour and asked if he could take it to bed, he reads for half an hour every night but usually fiction. Following morning (yesterday) he was asking permission to access some of the links, for inspiration. His behaviour and self-awareness has already improved, but also for his mum to see under cons the words Frustration and Retaliation is already helping her to have meaningful conversations with Alex and his teacher. So thank you."

"I attended a branding workshop that was run by Sid Madge, who at the very end mentioned the Meee Programme and this book! I downloaded the Kindle version, started reading it, then realised I needed the physical copy too! The bite-size chapters make this book an easy read, you don't drown in a huge chapter of information/motivation/tips or advice. Instead you can pick your chapter, take a minute to read it and then act!"

"This little book is brilliantly concise. Sid Madge has the ability to impart a range of very easy to understand messages in 60 bite-sized chapters.

"I loved that he gives links to some free sites that help the reader to develop areas of interest."

"The concept of a daily message isn't new, but this has inspired me to investigate a number of new areas."

"This is not a read once and cast aside book, I will be

dipping back in randomly every day to maintain positivity and develop my own potential."

"Who wants to stay calm? Not me, get inspired and excited and get out there and make a difference. Sid Madge has opened the door and showed us the way."

"A concise brilliant book to read and to then dip in and out of!

"Clearly written by someone who has seen the need first hand."

"So relevant to all of us with something for everyone."

"What a delightful and uplifting book. The content is both easily accessible and profound at once."

"So much to treasure here and tools that can be immediately applied and worked on for the rest of your life."

"A simple book.... about life! Written in short concise passages it is intended as a guide to help get the most out of our existence. I read it alongside my other reading which I rarely ever do. I did that because I wanted to absorb the advice and reflect on it. Recommended :)"

"A wonderful small resource, full of big ideas aimed at both individuals and practitioners alike. A useful addition to the library for anyone who works with people in a well-being/mental health setting or has an interest in Positive Psychology."

From our Employment Programme:

"The Meee Programme changed and saved my life, it truly is the miracle I was looking for."

"I am feeling so positive since doing your course it has been non-stop all good for me."

"I think Meee and my future was the best exercise because it's made me think about what I want and need to do in life to be happy and successful. I've learned that I need to learn to love myself in order to be truly happy."

"I am more positive about who I am."

"I like the fact this course gets you thinking."

"I found the team to be easy to get along with, highly approachable and helpful."

"It has inspired me to figure out where I am in life and has helped gain confidence."

"The team were very open and relatable. This helped me relax and take in more information so I could get the most out of the course."

"It has inspired me to do my qualification to work in a nursery."

"The Meee Programme has encouraged me to be who I am."

"The Meee Programme has got me to realise what I like and to get a career."

"I feel like I am going to achieve what I want to be in the future because the Meee Programme has helped me."

"It has inspired me to read more books like Adam Braun's *The Promise of a Pencil.*"

"Made me relax more."

"It made me want to do voluntary work to gain experience and confidence before having a permanent job."

"It has shown me how to be more confident."

"It has inspired me to make time for myself."

"To look at going on a computer course."

"I understand how to control my emotions more."

"It inspired me not to be lazy and practice my passion (cooking)."

"I am now going to college to study catering."

"It has inspired me to become a better self, and I will be using the reading list to help achieve this."

"It has inspired me to push to get my coaching qualifications."

"I feel more confident to approach different people and that there is a range of different jobs and work experience opportunities."

"I now have a better idea of what I want to achieve."

"I must do more research on different childcare careers, so I can find something appropriate."

"Yes I found this (the Meee workshops) extremely helpful so anything else you offer will be grabbed with both hands. If there is any role I can apply my skills/strengths to, I would be happy to help."

"I'm inspired to move forward with my life and to overcome my weakness or at least be able to accept them and stop them holding me back."

"I feel more positive about the future now and sad it has come to the end. I feel inspired and confident."

"Brilliant, insightful, helpful."

"It was different to other courses I have been on because it didn't focus all about getting into work but learning about yourself & everyday struggles/happiness."

"The course has been excellent at helping with helping me discover myself and made me feel much more comfortable with who I am."

"I honestly enjoyed all aspects of this course, it has widened my view on life and made me aware to my options in life."

"It has been a confidence boost and very helpful."

"I definitely feel so much happier now that I've done the course."

"I have really enjoyed the course so much, I feel happier now every time it comes to the end of the day I constantly have a smile on my face which is great."

"Having bipolar disorder and anxiety I have found the Meee course more inspiring at uplifting than any of the counselling I've done and depression courses."

"Helpful, polite, understanding sympathetic but not patronising. AMAZING."

"I would like to support Meee in some way as I think it's an amazing idea and it has really helped me."

"I feel closer to writing my books and more able to look for work."

"I just thought I'd let you know that I've successfully started my new job as a personal assistant! Everything is going really, really well and most importantly I'm really enjoying it! I feel like a better person and I don't think I ever would of found the confidence in myself to go for such a job if it wasn't for Sid and you! Made me realise what I can actually achieve and pushed myself further to get to where I am now, so thank you to both of you and best of luck with the Programme, I hope many more people can also say the same!" Xx

"I have seen a great impact on A, he was smiling and engaged without being prompted when I met him this week. I met with B today and she is so fired up and raring to go with a determination I haven't seen before. I asked her to rate her confidence level from 0–10 before and after your course and she said she was a 2 going in and now feels she is a 9!!! C – wow – he could barely speak when I met him the for the first time the Friday week before the course, he couldn't stop talking about it."

"It was great in the group I loved it."

"The customers are so inspired and I can't thank you enough."

"The exercise that helped me mostly was the strength and weakness.. When I first started on the course I was in a dark place and I could tell you so many weaknesses I had but ask me to write a positive that was hard ... Also the timeline from birth to where I was and where I wanted to be. I've always had dreams working in hotels running them etc. Without the course I wouldn't of had the confidence to climb out of the big hole I was in .. I have a job in a hotel now starting from the bottom and I'm going to work my way up and I don't care how long it takes. I didn't realize how strong I was till I went on the course. To fight drink and drugs and a mentally and physically abusive ex mates that treated me like a slave and a built in babysitter in my last job I got away from all that but still felt weak. After the Meee course I felt so much better about myself and so much more positive about me ..My life .."

"I cant thank you enough for helping me realize who I am and helped me climb out of the hole I dug myself .. The Meee course was amazing and trust me I was dreading it I thought it would be boring as hell but given the chance I'd love to do it all over again." :-) x

"I need some new sunglasses because the future is so bright. I could quite easily have given up hope of scaffolding full time again but I took the knock backs on the chin, kept the faith and ended up smiling again. It's good to hear from you Sid and I hope you will continue to inspire and find the CAN DO we know is in everyone like you did with our team. So long until the next time my friend and long may MEEE continue to succeed and grow."

"Hope all is well with you just want to say how much this course has helped me build my confidence so much so I've gotten a job after applying at the jobs fair so I'm really pleased with myself but couldn't of done it without you..."

"Keep inspiring people the way you did me, best of luck with your programme for the future, happy smiley Vinney."

From our Enterprise Programme:

"Thanks so much for Tuesday. Al and I really found it very informative and energising! U were brilliant and we were really touched by your kindness. We have adopted JBN! Lol. Take care and thanks again."

"It was a thoroughly enjoyable, inspirational and useful day yesterday. You obviously have a great passion for sharing your knowledge and enthusiasm and I really loved how the day went, with so much interaction and little swerves off the path yet always brought back, in a timely way, to the subject in question. It was such an interesting mix of experiences and businesses."

"The workshop was a total eye-opener for me trying to set up a new business. Sid delivered his valuable knowledge around branding in an enthralling and powerful manner. I not only left with some actionable tasks to help build my brand but also a new excitement around exactly how I am going to grow my audience and business. No matter what stage you are in your career, chances are you need this workshop!"

"I've attended a few marketing workshops - one really boring, another very entertaining, but this had lots to offer - neither boring nor superfluous. Good information expressed directly and offering meaning to my business. It was inspiring and jerked me out of my marketing coma. After the event I felt less like a waffle and more like Cracker!"

"I'll be completing the worksheets for sure and it's really made me think about my company values and how important they are to my business.

"I'm about to employ my first employee so it's inspired me to get my company values embedded from the start!"

"I really got so much from Wednesday and made the connection with how business, people and energy can all combine to create positive change in the world, and that I can/am actually be part of it all. Penny dropping moment :0) yippeee!"

"I cannot thank you enough for just being 'YOU', you really did bring back my motivation and passion for business! Just what I needed!"

From our Family Programme:

"If you have a choice between being right and being kind, choose to be kind, this course has helped me to do that."

"My son has realised he is not the only person at the school who struggles, he is not alone anymore."

"The Meee Programme is happiness."

"After the course our family has learnt to love, help and support one another."

From our Meee Education Programme:

"My Sixth Form tutor signed me up for the Meee Programme that was running and I was so surprised by how much it made me change the way I view life, the education system, other students around me, and me. Hearing that others see me as a genuine, loving person with a cool, unique foreign name really boosted my confidence. They saw the good in me, when I didn't, and I will be always thankful for that!"

"Thank you so much, you were so friendly and I learned lots of new things. It was also so much fun!"

"Can we do that everyday."

"Thank you for coming and teaching us new things, it was amazing!"

- "Thank you for making this fun, I learned a lot!"
- "It was amazing."
- "I loved it."
- "Sid and Tia did an excellent job at teaching me self-belief."
- "Meee has made me realise I need to push myself."
- "The course has taught me to relax more."
- "The Meee Programme shows you how to be grateful for everything."

Staff

- "Helped me be more aware of ensuring the happiness and enjoyment of the children (and myself!)"
- "Keep our focus on the children in every way – both emotionally and educationally."
- "To be more inclusive, help children build confidence. Work as a team."
- "Not to worry about silly things that may never happen."
- "A great reminder on how important our role as teachers in school is, and how important it is that school needs to be a happy/caring environment."

"They have a fantastic way with the children. They make the sessions enjoyable and the pupils feel comfortable and at ease to express themselves and their thoughts on the topics discussed."

"The sessions are full of great stories, inspirational messages and opportunities to look at everyday life in a different way."

"It is clear from the pupils responses that they were fully engaged with the sessions and would take part again at the drop of a hat."

"Sid's passion and down to earth approach to staff development was refreshing and had a remarkable effect on my staff's drive and enthusiasm...he revived in them the reason they came into the profession in the first place."

"It's helped me look at my work life in a different way and hopefully be a better teaching assistant."

"To be more inclusive, help children build confidence. Work as a team."

"Not to worry about silly things that may never happen."

Students

"It inspired me to work more towards university."

"My son has never enjoyed a school session like this in his life. He cried when he got home, as he said someone finally gets me."

- "It's OK to be me."
- "Fantastic programme recommend it to anyone."
- "It has inspired me to be happier."
- "Thank you for helping me be me."
- "This should be in every school in the world."
- "Why hasn't this been invented before?"
- "Meee has been really helpful and now I feel more confident."
- "I loved every minute of it."
- "I am enough."

From our Prison Programme:

- "The Meee Programme...Opened my mind and my heart to loving myself and seeing the potential in myself and others have! Uplifting and thought provoking!"
- "This course has done more for me in these last 5 days, than the last 9 years of my sentence... you don't even know what you've done for me. Thank you from depths of my heart!"
- "Whole heartedly exceptional, mind blowing and life changing. You both deserve a medal."

"Sid and Jamie are brilliant at what they do. They are really inspirational, happy and enthusiastic and are brilliant at making others feel good and optimistic about their futures."

"Really uplifting and the best people for the job."

"The MEEE Programme...Opened my mind and my heart to loving myself and seeing the potential myself and others have! Uplifting and though provoking!"

"An excellent course which was delivered extremely well."

"I appreciate everything they've done for me. They were all very helpful. If I was down they would bring me up!"

"Very clear in their ways and shared interesting stuff, made me realise a lot."

"I think they bring a very good vibe to the prisoners and really could and will make a difference."

"Brilliant! Really enthusiastic and want to believe in the people they are working with."

"It's inspired me to help other people. I've now become a council rep on my wing."

"I think my timeline (future) was a brilliant exercise for me because it has got me thinking about what I want to be doing when I get released. I thought I knew what I wanted to do, now I believe I can do better than what I originally planned for my future."

"Brilliant course, really enjoyed it."

"This is the first course I have ever completed in prison. I have never stayed longer than a day on any course and I stayed on this one for all 4 days."

"This course should be in every prison."

"I think it will be an excellent idea to have this national across all prisons."

"Fantastic programme recommend it to anyone."

Sid Madge and the Meee Programme

A brand strategist with over 30 years' experience, Sid Madge has channelled his expertise to found the Meee Programme – an initiative to help people understand and believe in themselves.

It all began in 2009 when Sid chose to relocate from London to a remote corner of north Wales. He set himself a challenge: to build his own branding agency, in the middle of nowhere, knowing no one. But it turned out that this was just the start of a bigger, even more exciting challenge.

While running a workshop at a local school, Sid asked pupils to pick one word to describe themselves. The results were a real eye opener. 15 per cent used terms like 'freak, 'weirdo' and 'misfit'. In fact, so many people of all ages had a negative self-image that Sid felt compelled to take action and the Meee Programme was born.

Since May 2015 he's been developing tools and delivering workshops to help people believe in themselves. Bringing together Sid's in-depth branding expertise with knowledge from psychology, neuroscience, education, branding and sociology, the Meee Programme encourages everyone to recognise and believe in their abilities.

In March 2015, Sid was invited to Number 10 Downing Street to present the Meee Programme to Lord Young, who endorsed it as 'a great initiative'. In three years Sid and the Meee team have delivered talks, workshops and classes to over 1,000 people, working with businesses, job centres, rehabilitation centres, prisons and educational establishments across the UK.

Sid's next goal is to bring the benefits of the Meee Programme to everyone, everywhere. Covering Education, Employment and Enterprise, Meee has the power to transform the way people think about their life and the role they can play.

As mentioned on page 23, take a minute to write down (opposite) your top six priorities for work tomorrow and order them by importance.

Tomorrow, when you go to work, start on this list and follow Ivy Lee's advice. Implementing this system is a sure-fire way to increase your productivity, and when you continue to replicate this approach, week on week, it shouldn't be long before people start to notice!

1. ______________________________

____

2. ______________________________

____

3. ______________________________

____

4. ______________________________

____

5. ______________________________

____

6. ______________________________

____

As mentioned on page 59, write down your 6 most satisfying achievements from the last 10 years.

1. ____________________

2. ____________________

3. ____________________

4. ____________________

5. ____________________

6. ____________________

Now re-energise your efforts and dot down what you'd like to achieve over the next 10 years.

1. ____________________

2. ____________________

3. ____________________

4. ____________________

5. ____________________

6. ____________________

NOTES SECTION

To take the next stage on your journey watch our free webinar at **www.meee.global/webinar** for many more practical hints and tips.

• • • • • • • • • • • • •

Plus, if you enjoyed **Meee In A Work Minute**, then the inspirational **Meee In A Minute,** and **Meee In A Family Minute** books are available from the same series. Purchase your copies at: **meeebooks.com**

All publications are available in paperback, e-book and audiobook.